D0611179

CROSSCURRENTS *Modern Critiques*

CROSSCURRENTS *Modern Critiques*
Harry T. Moore, *General Editor*

Frank Rosengarten

Vasco Pratolini

THE DEVELOPMENT
OF A SOCIAL NOVELIST

WITH A PREFACE BY

Harry T. Moore

Carbondale and Edwardsville

SOUTHERN ILLINOIS UNIVERSITY PRESS

To my wife, Lillian,
whose love and
encouragement were indispensable
to me in the writing of this book

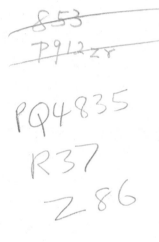

PREFACE

VASCO PRATOLINI is best known in the United States for his 1947 book, Cronache di poveri amanti (A Tale of Poor Lovers), but his other novels also deserve to be read, as the present volume emphatically demonstrates.

To many of us outsiders, Italian fascism seemed unimportant beside its German cousin, nazism. Those of us who traveled through Mussolini's Italy, uninformed about the reality of events, are known for admiring the way the trains ran on time; and certainly we saw nothing that resembled the activities that we heard were being carried on at the time by the Nazi storm troopers. And at the time of the Second World War, our advancing troops found no such horrors as the German corpse camps with their gas ovens. Recently there have even been biographies purporting to show that Mussolini wasn't such a bad guy, after all.

But life under dictatorship, under totalitarian control, is full of suffering and evil. Pratolini shows us just how bad conditions were in Mussolini's time—these novels take us into the back streets of Florence, the working-class quarter into which few tourists strayed; the books show us the compulsion and brutality the Fascists exercised there. It was, under the surface, a horrible time, and Pratolini is its historian, using his own experiences and those of others to make his points with the emotional force that is one of the great properties of fiction.

Not that Pratolini was always an anti-Fascist. A poor boy, son of a father wounded at the battle of the Pieave in the First World War, Pratolini in his youth believed in fascism; he was even, as Mr. Rosengarten points out in the present book, a zealot. But he changed, and his change is the true subject of Mr. Rosengarten's interesting and valuable study, which is subtitled "The Development of a Social Novelist." During the war, Pratolini had become a sufficiently convinced anti-Fascist to be an important member of the Resistance. As Mr. Rosengarten points out, Pratolini's one-time Fascist allegiance was sometimes used against him after the war, but his reformation was a convincing one, as his writing shows.

Mr. Rosengarten deals extensively—and necessarily—with Pratolini's biography in the first part of this book. Then he examines Pratolini the author, particularly the writer of fiction. He shows how the events of his life have shaped his work, and discusses the other authors who have influenced him, writers as divergent as Victor Hugo and the medieval Florentine chroniclers. Mr. Rosengarten then treats Pratolini's work critically, explicating as well as evaluating, and what he says gives the fullest account we have yet had in English of one of the outstanding European authors of our time, a man who has grappled with the most difficult problems of this epoch and has written of them in a manner both local and universal. Pratolini has much to say to us all in this exploding world, and Mr. Rosengarten provides a lucid, thorough, and important guide to his work.

HARRY T. MOORE

Southern Illinois University
March 21, 1965

CONTENTS

INTRODUCTION

VASCO PRATOLINI is one of a group of writers who rose to prominence in Italy in the years immediately following the end of the second World War. A Florentine of working class origin, he belongs to what has been referred to as "the Fascist generation." Born in 1913, he was nine years old at the outset of the Fascist epoch, twenty-two at the time of the Ethiopian campaign, and barely thirty when the fortunes of war divided Italy into two armed camps.

In 1943, like Elio Vittorini, Cesare Pavese, Carlo Bernari, and other writers and intellectuals of his generation, Pratolini made a dramatic repudiation of fascism when he joined the Resistance and affiliated with the Italian Communist Party. Pratolini's participation in the Resistance marked a decisive turning point in his career. It was this experience that helped him to emerge from the spiritual isolation in which he had languished since the outbreak of World War II, and that provided him with a rich variety of themes for the novels and short stories he was to write in the years to come.

Pratolini has been the subject of innumerable reviews and articles, quite a few lengthy critical essays, and one major study by Alberto Asor Rosa. Rosa's *Vasco Pratolini* (Rome, 1958) differs from this study in a number of important respects. In the first place, there are many aspects of Pratolini's career which Rosa, writing as an Italian for an Italian audience, felt he could take for granted, but which are of vital importance to a proper understanding of Pratolini's artistic development. For example, Rosa disposes of Pratolini's youthful involvement in the Fascist movement in less than two pages, and alludes only briefly to the writings he produced during the 1930's. Yet, as I hope to show, Pratolini's involvement in fascism and the creative and critical writings he published in various periodicals during the 1930's cannot be dismissed as forming part of his "pre-history," as they are by Rosa. Secondly, this study attempts a more thorough examination of those of Pratolini's critical writings that illuminate aspects of his creative work at various stages of his career. Thirdly, Rosa's essays on Pratolini's works, while often brilliant in themselves, are not unified by a central idea. Although he indicates clearly the existence of a developmental pattern in Pratolini's art, he does not deal with it directly. Yet Pratolini's steady evolution towards the novel of social realism embedded in historical fact is undoubtedly the most striking characteristic of his career.

As already noted, some important essays dealing with diverse facets of Pratolini's career have appeared. Among the most significant are Francesco Flora's essay in *Scrittori italiani contemporanei* (Pisa, 1952), Maria Sticco's in *Il romanzo italiano contemporaneo* (Rome, 1953), Sergio Pacifici's chapter on Pratolini in his *A Guide to Contemporary Italian Literature* (Cleveland, 1962), Fulvio Longobardi's *Vasco Pratolini* (Milan, 1964), and a series of perceptive articles by Carlo Salinari, Carlo Muscetta, and Piero Pucci in the June, 1956, issue of *Societa*. In addition, I have relied as general guides, especially in regard to the post-war period, on Giorgio Pullini's *Il romanzo italiano del dopoguerra* (Milan, 1961), Giacinto Spagnoletti's *Romanzieri italiani del nostro secolo* (Turin, 1957), Angelo Paoluzi's *La letteratura della Resistenza* (Florence, 1956), Luigi Russo's *I narratori, 1850–1950* (Milan, 1951), Enrico Falqui's *Prosatori e narratori del novecento italiano* (Turin, 1950), and Carlo Bo's *Inchiesta sul neorealismo* (Turin, 1951).

Pratolini's career lends itself particularly well to chronological treatment. Each of the five chapters that comprise this study corresponds to a distinct phase of his development. Chapter 1 describes Pratolini's childhood and adolescence in Florence. In chapters 2 through 5, prior to my thematic analyses of the works themselves, I aim primarily to provide the reader with a frame of reference within which to interpret Pratolini's art. In accordance with this aim, I discuss important aspects of the cultural climate of the period under study, and examine Pratolini's literary sources and affinities, his critical ideas, and his responses to or participation in various literary and political movements. All of the passages quoted from Pratolini's writings have been translated.

I WISH TO EXPRESS MY THANKS to the entire staff of the Casa Italiana for encouragement and useful suggestions. I owe a special debt of gratitude to Professor Olga Ragusa, who helped me to understand some of the basic problems, techniques and aims of literary scholarship.

For permission to cite passages from translations I wish to thank the Orion Press, Inc. for *Two Brothers*; A. A. Wyn, Inc. for *The Naked Streets*; Hamish Hamilton Ltd. for *A Tale of Poor Lovers*; and Arnoldo Mondadori Editore and Pocket Books for *The Girls of San Frediano*.

FRANK ROSENGARTEN

Western Reserve University
January 15, 1965

Vasco Pratolini

THE DEVELOPMENT OF
A SOCIAL NOVELIST

1 THE EARLY YEARS
(1913–1932)

THE SECOND DECADE of this century ushered in a period of grave political and social crisis in Italy. The internal political conflicts engendered by the outbreak of the First World War reflected the fundamental disunity of the Italian people and foreshadowed the more serious dissension which, in the immediate postwar years, was to lead to the rise and triumph of the Fascist movement. Although technically victorious, Italy, in reality, emerged from the First World War as a vanquished nation. Six hundred thousand of her young men died in battle. Many of those who returned to their homes were unable to find employment. Victory parades and patriotic oratory had little meaning for the millions of Italians who were even more impoverished in 1918 than they had been before the advent of the war.

Profiting by the confusion and widespread disillusionment which affected every segment of Italian society at the war's end, the newly formed Fascist party became a force to be reckoned with. At first it made its most direct appeal to the war veterans. But in 1921, a series of general strikes, the formation of workers' councils in the factories of Piedmont and Lombardy, and the founding of the Italian Communist party, marked a sudden upsurge of working class militancy. To counter the threat of a "bolshevized" Italy, landowners and industrialists began to rely more and more heavily on the Fascist "squads" as instruments with which to protect their economic interests. By 1925, because of the inherent weaknesses of the Italian parliamentary system, the persuasiveness of Mussolini, whose vehemently nationalistic speeches and writings appealed to ever-widening numbers of people from all social classes, and the inability of liberal and left-wing anti-Fascist groups to solve their own internal problems, the Fascist party seized virtual control of the Italian government.

It is against the background of the events briefly alluded to above that Pratolini's early years are to be seen.[1] He belonged to a family which lived continuously on the edge of penury, so that the war for him did not mean patriotic songs, slogans, and parades, but rather hunger and bread lines. Throughout his childhood he looked upon the war and its tragic aftermath as incontrovertible facts of life which he and his family, as well as all the poor people of Florence, were destined to endure. He understood the meaning of fatalism long before the word itself became a part of his vocabulary.

The rise of fascism, on the other hand, symbolized to young Pratolini the beginning of a new and exciting era in Italian history. Fascism first presented itself to his consciousness as a movement which would vindicate the rights of the poor and the oppressed through a program of national regeneration. The exploits of the Florentine blackshirts, who were known throughout Italy for their fanaticism, gave him the feeling that events did not have to be passively endured, but rather that they could be created by men of courage and determination. Fascism signified change, revolution, and above all, action. It was precisely the Fascists' capacity for decisive action and defiance of the customary amenities of parliamentary procedure that first won his admiration and allegiance. For young Pratolini, the First World War meant suffering, despair, fatalism, whereas fascism symbolized action, hope, and voluntarism. The tension produced in him by these two diametrically opposed sets of emotions accounts in large measure for the curious admixture of fatalism and revolutionary optimism that characterizes many of his writings.

Vasco Pratolini was born on October 19, 1913, and spent the first seven years of his life in a small, cold-water flat at 1, via de' Magazzini. Via de' Magazzini is one of the many streets in the center of Florence which, despite their proximity to Piazza della Signoria and the presumed birthplace of Dante, are rarely frequented by tourists. Indeed, there is little on this narrow, cobblestone street to arouse the interest of a foreign visitor.

In 1915, Pratolini's father, Ugo, was drafted into the army. He did not return to his family until 1918, when he was discharged with a small pension granted him as a result of wounds received in the battle of the Piave, and a medal for bravery in action. During his infancy and early childhood, Pratolini was cared for by his mother, Nella, and by his maternal grandparents, Pio and Rosa Casati. Pio and Rosa were both of peasant origin and were endowed with a stubborn tenacity and the courage to struggle against hardships, qualities which their daughter did not possess. Unlike Rosa, who was illiterate throughout her life, Pio took great pride in his ability to read and write, and was regarded by his friends as a man of astute political judgment and strong Socialist convictions.

In 1917 Ugo was wounded and wrote letter after letter imploring his wife to come and visit him. For the first and only time in her life, Nella left Florence and journeyed north to Milan, where Ugo was convalescing. It was during those few days of intimacy that their second child was conceived. Almost immediately after her return to Florence, Nella fell into a state of severe melancholia. This malady, from which she had suffered even as a young girl, was now aggravated by her second pregnancy, the absence of her husband, anxieties caused by the precariously delicate health of Vasco, and the daily pressures of domestic responsibilities. At the age of four, Pratolini was already immersed in a world of anxiety and suffering from which he would emerge only after many years of struggle. Nella could not satisfy his need for love. She grew constantly more withdrawn and uncommunicative. Occasionally she would become somewhat more expansive, but essentially she was an aloof and melancholy person. Up to the moment of her death in 1918, only a few months after the birth of her second son, Ferruccio, she regarded herself as a victim of evil forces over which neither she nor anyone else could exercise control.

Nella's death intensified Pratolini's need for affection,

a need which could only be partially satisfied by his father and grandparents. Ugo was young and resilient, and after the first shock of grief had passed, he plunged back into work and spent his evenings talking and drinking with friends. Pio spent some of his free time with his grandson, but he was an old man who craved solitude and repose. Rosa, therefore, was the person upon whom devolved the responsibility of attending to the boy's needs. An obstinate, stern, hard-working woman, she found it difficult to express her feelings. Whenever possible, after doing the chores assigned to him by his grandmother, young Vasco escaped to the nearby squares, returning home at twilight to Rosa's inevitable reproaches. In 1920, after a series of bitter quarrels with Rosa, Ugo decided to remarry. It was at this point in his childhood that Vasco began to discover an element of strong rebelliousness in his character, for he refused to accept Erina, his stepmother, openly expressed his resentments against his father, and scorned his grandmother's constant admonishments to avoid the company of "ill-bred ruffians."

In 1921 Pratolini's parents moved to via dei Pepi, in the working class quarter of Santa Croce, while his grandparents remained at the apartment on via de' Magazzini. For the next several years, Pratolini spent three or four days of the week with his parents, the rest with his grandparents. He hated his stepmother, and invented an extraordinary number of excuses for staying away from via dei Pepi. On weekends, he often accompanied his grandmother on her weekly visits to the home of a wealthy English lord. One of the lord's servant girls had taken pity on little Ferruccio, Pratolini's younger brother, when she learned that his mother was dead and that he was being cared for by a wet nurse. She implored Ugo to give his infant son over to her care, and spoke of the advantages that Ferruccio would have as the adopted son of a wealthy English gentleman. Ugo had at first rejected the idea, but when the girl threatened to commit suicide, he acceded to her wishes.[2]

Thus Ferruccio grew up in an entirely different world from that of Vasco. He was pampered and doted on by the English lord and his majordomo, and utterly spoiled by the servant girl's assiduous attentions. Vasco, on the other hand, had begun to develop that spirit of rugged independence and self-reliance which is typical of boys who must learn to fend for themselves. But if Ferruccio's spirit of independence was undermined by indulgent adults, Vasco ran the dangers of children left to their own resources. He became an habitual truant, and attended classes only when the subject being studied was of particular interest to him. The principal demanded to know why he had absented himself so often from class. Since Vasco had no adequate answer, he was suspended, and ultimately expelled in 1924, when he was barely eleven years old. The main explanation for Pratolini's truancy was that he had joined a gang of boys known throughout the quarter of Santa Croce for their boldness, their rebelliousness, and their numerous escapades, often of a frankly delinquent nature—petty thievery and pickpocketing were two of their regular activities. But the gang also had its virtues, among which was a strong spirit of group solidarity.

Very early in his association with his friends, Pratolini acquired the reputation of being the most knowledgeable among them. He admired their physical courage and spirit of adventure; they esteemed his intelligence. It is difficult to explain the development of Pratolini's intellectual curiosity which his friends so admired. Up to the age of fifteen or sixteen, his friendships were limited to the boys and girls of Santa Croce, all of whom were as poor and as ignorant as he. Pratolini himself attributes the first awakening of his intellectual curiosity to the omnipresence of literary and historical landmarks in Florence. Doubtless his grandfather, Pio, who respected learning, deserves some credit for Vasco's early interest in books and ideas. An episode from Pratolini's story, "The Early Life of Sapienza," gives some indication of his first readings. In the following passage Pratolini describes his efforts at the tender age of thirteen to start a library for the use of the "community" of boys to which he belonged:

The exploits of the "community" yielded money, which I found myself forced to spend immediately: I was spied on and intimidated by my parents, and was therefore unable to bring the money home with me. Consequently, I proposed to the community the idea of a library, which I offered to pay for myself. The books were kept at our "headquarters," which was a cellar we rented from an itinerant fruit vendor who shared it with us. Anthologies of Salgari and Poe in cheap popular editions, of Motta and Zola, and entire collections, issue by issue, of the adventures of Nat Pinkerton and Lord Lister, of Petrosino, Rocambole and Ricimera; I had ordered books about thieves and detectives of great style and honor, yet they were of only moderate interest to my friends, who avoided reading the stories and placed their faith in the summaries I gave of them.[3]

The adventure stories of Salgari, the strange fantasies of Poe, Zola's accounts of Parisian low-life, and an endless succession of detective and crime stories—these comprised the essential substance of Pratolini's early literary experiences. But at the age of fifteen or sixteen, his readings assumed a more serious character. Aside from lighter fare, such as *Pinocchio*, whose pungent wit he vastly enjoyed, and the science fiction of Jules Verne, he read Jack London's *Martin Eden*, Dostoevsky's *Crime and Punishment*, and the short stories of De Maupassant, all of which he purchased in cheap popular editions published by the firm of Sonzogno. Even more significant than his contacts with this disparate group of authors was his reading of *The Divine Comedy*, which was the object of his first really serious and systematic study of a literary work, and of *La Vita Nuova*, whose occult ambiguities and tender portrayal of young love stimulated his youthful imagination. In all likelihood he read these works with only partial understanding of their multi-leveled and symbolic meanings, yet certainly the long hours he spent pondering the verse and prose of Dante, and the search for historical sources which the reading of Dante necessitated, contributed to the development of a serious and dedicated attitude towards literature.

In 1927, following the death of his grandfather and increasingly acrimonious quarrels with his parents, Pratolini moved with his grandmother to an apartment on via del Corno, an obscure corner of the ancient maze of streets and alleyways which surround Palazzo Vecchio. From 1927 to 1929 he lived among the workers, artisans, and street vendors who appear in his best known novel, *Cronache di poveri amanti*. In the summer of 1929 Pratolini's grandmother became ill and was taken to a home for the aged, and a year later Pratolini moved across the Arno to via Toscanella in the working-class quarter of San Frediano. He was then doing general clerical work for the Italian branch office of a French soap company. He spent much of his free time in the Florentine public library, and it was there he continued his discoveries of the "great books" of Italian literature. The chronicles of Compagni and Villani, the tales of Boccaccio and Sacchetti, and the historical narratives of Machiavelli were among the books that first awoke in Pratolini the strong sense of identification with Florentine literary traditions which was later to be of such decisive importance in his artistic and general intellectual development.

In 1932 Pratolini made his initial entrance into Florentine cultural and political life, when he began contributing articles of political commentary, short stories and prose poems to *Il Bargello*, the official organ of the Florentine *Fasci di Combattimento*. Poverty and the obligations of work were no hindrance to him at this stage of his career, for he was sustained by a sure sense of latent powers, and by an ardent faith in fascism as a purifying and revolutionary force in Italian society. For young Pratolini, Mussolini's regime represented at once the triumph of order and social discipline over capitalist exploitation, the beginning of a new era of imperial splendor, the enfranchisement of Italian youth, and the possibility of a great rebirth of artistic and literary endeavor. Fascism, he thought, was a new, vital, revolutionary force in Italian life. For this reason, the articles he began publishing in *Il Bargello* in 1932 were often signed: "Vasco Pratolini, a young Fascist from beyond the Arno."

THE YOUNG FASCIST WRITER
(1932–1939)

1 *Art and Society*

During the years 1932 to 1939 Pratolini's life was marked by a succession of physical and moral crises. Although he read, studied, and wrote with a kind of passionate intensity, often characteristic of the self-taught man, he also worked an eight hour day and frequently spent his nights gambling and carousing with friends. Because of his absorption in work and pleasure, but mainly because of his impoverished condition, he ate irregularly. In March, 1935, he discovered that he had contracted tuberculosis. The illness was fortunately still in an incipient phase, but he had to spend the next two years at a sanitarium in Arco, a small town in the Italian Dolomites situated about five miles from Lake Garda.

In 1954, in the preface to "Diario di Villa Rosa," a diary he kept during his two years of confinement at Arco, Pratolini confessed that, before becoming ill in 1935, he had been a brash, combative young man sure of his Fascist convictions and disdainful of everyone who did not view the world as he did. After his recovery two years later, he was a wiser, more temperate person:

> They were two decisive years, in every sense. I was violent; I became submissive; I learned to fear death, to respect life. Above all the life of other people because I had learned to value my own.[1]

Soon after his return to Florence in the summer of 1937 Pratolini went to work in the make-up room of *Il Bargello*, a job he held until August, 1938, when, together with the poet Alfonso Gatto, he founded a literary review named *Campo di Marte*.

In August, 1939, Pratolini and Gatto were forced to suspend publication of *Campo di Marte*. The review had not met with the official approval of the Fascist Ministry of Culture. It was reported that *Campo di Marte* had been suspended by "mutual consent." But there was a practical motive behind Pratolini's acceptance of the phrase "mutual consent": he had already decided to leave Florence to apply for a position with the Ministry of Education in Rome. He had been rejected for military service and was in urgent need of stable employment. A few weeks after his arrival in Rome in October, 1939, Pratolini presented his letters of recommendation to the ministry and was soon at work on his first assignment, setting up an archive on contemporary Italian art. His job consisted of gathering biographical information on modern Italian painters and writing short critical studies of their works.[2]

Throughout the 1930's Pratolini's literary and political values were shaped in large measure by particular personalities and groups then prominent in Florentine cultural circles. It is necessary, therefore, to describe briefly the character of the Florentine cultural milieu in which his early development took place.

The policies and pronouncements of the Fascist government elicited varying responses from the different groups which composed the Florentine cultural world in the early 1930's. One extremely important group, which gravitated around the magazine *Solaria*, assumed an attitude of aristocratic detachment from all issues and ideas that were not exclusively "literary." The editors of the magazine *Il Frontespizio* declared themselves in general agreement with the aims of the Fascist state, although they felt that the regime was not making a sufficiently intensive effort to inculcate traditional religious values into the youth of Italy. *L'Universale* and *Il Bargello*, on the other hand, enthusiastically endorsed every aspect of Fascist policy and doctrine.

Solaria was founded in January, 1926, and its co-editors, Alberto Carocci and Giansiro Ferrata, contributed an introductory statement of purpose to the first number.

After making pointed reference to the unpolitical and eclectic nature of their interests, they stated, "Solaria comes into being without a precise program and with an inheritance that is not to be disdained." [3] In saying that *Solaria* was building on "an inheritance that is not to be disdained," Carocci and Ferrata were referring to the Roman literary review *La Ronda*, which had been published from 1919 to 1922. *La Ronda's* effort to inculcate respect for Italian literary and cultural traditions was to continue as one of the primary functions of the new Florentine review. Like Riccardo Bacchelli, Antonio Baldini, Vincenzo Cardarelli, and Emilio Cecchi, who in their writings for *La Ronda* had sought to bring their readers into contact with European rather than only Italian literary movements, and who viewed literature as an autonomous intellectual discipline that ought not to be subjected to political or social pressures, Carocci and Ferrata defended the concept of art as the expression of its creator's unique personality and vision.

The introductory statement indicated a definite receptivity to diverse literary currents on the part of Carocci and Ferrata. They referred admiringly to the verbal experimentation of Virginia Woolf, the psychological realism of Italo Svevo, the dramatic intensity of O'Neill's plays, and in general showed their awareness of the many new forms and possibilities of literary expression that were available to the modern writer. This receptivity to diverse literary currents on the part of *Solaria's* editors represented a significant trend in contemporary Florentine life, a trend which helped Pratolini, Elio Vittorini, Romano Bilenchi, and other writers of "the Fascist generation" eventually to liberate themselves from a narrowly doctrinaire conception of literature. By bringing foreign authors of seminal importance to the attention of its readers, *Solaria* helped to counteract the pressure of cultural chauvinism which fascism had brought to bear on the Italian literary world. *Solaria* ceased publication in 1934. Three years later most of its collaborators participated in the founding of *Letteratura*, which continued to provide translations and critical studies of foreign authors, and which reaffirmed the principles of the autonomy and inviolability of artistic expression.

As opposed to *Solaria*'s predominant interest in literary values, *Il Frontespizio*'s director Piero Bargellini, and the most frequent contributors, Giovanni Papini, Ardengo Soffici, Domenico Giuliotti, Mario Berti, and Nicola Lisi, were united by a desire to affirm the immortal and purifying power of catholicism. The editors of *Il Frontespizio* interpreted all contemporary social, political, and cultural phenomena *sub specie aeternitatis* and attributed what one of its collaborators called "the present superficiality of so much contemporary Italian literature" to the waning of religious passion in Italy's younger generation of writers.

In the early 1930's Pratolini had little in common with the aristocratic men of letters who gravitated around *Solaria* and had no interest whatever in the catholic message of *Il Frontespizio*. The men with whom he did share common beliefs and passions, and who exerted a direct influence on his vision of life, were the artists and writers who collaborated in bringing out still another Florentine literary review, *L'Universale*, which appeared from January, 1931, to August, 1935. Pratolini felt a close affinity with the editors of *L'Universale* because their faith in fascism was not attenuated by religious scruples, nor was it weakened by preoccupations with purely aesthetic values. For example, in an editorial entitled "Opinion," which appeared in the issue of June 3, 1931, the editors of *L'Universale* said: "Fascist art requires an imperialist policy in action, a heroism that is no longer spoken or described, but that is lived, and demands a potent and profound humanity in its creators." Perhaps the times were not yet propitious for the rebirth of a vital, dynamic literature in Italy, continued the author of "Opinion," but "we await from the times and from Mussolini the fulfillment of fascism's promise, the epic substance from which a great and true art will be born." [4] Characteristically enough, the editors of *L'Universale* suspended publication as soon as Italy invaded Ethiopia, since they felt that the chance to fight for their country was more important than pursuing their careers as writers.

Even more militantly nationalistic than *L'Universale* was *Il Bargello*, the official Florentine Fascist organ. Gioacchino Contri, its editor, took a personal interest in Pratolini and encouraged him to submit articles of political and literary commentary to the paper's *terza pagina*, which in accordance with a tradition of Italian journalism was devoted to literary and general cultural topics.[5] Hero worship of Mussolini constitutes one of the fundamental themes of Pratolini's early political writings in *Il Bargello*. In paying homage to a man who had been attacked and severely injured by anti-Fascists in July, 1922, and who had died in 1934 singing a hymn of praise to the Fascist regime, Pratolini wrote: "Today, I, a young Fascist, have paid homage to this unknown fallen compatriot—answering Present! for him, and committing myself by his example to serve the Duce and the Fatherland with faith and modesty to death."[6]

After the invasion of Ethiopia in October, 1935, Pratolini did not allow his confinement at the tuberculosis sanitarium to prevent him from participating spiritually in "the great enterprise." His reaction to Generoso Pucci's *Coi Negadi in Etiopia*, a study of economic and social conditions in Ethiopia, illustrates how completely he accepted the official justification which the Fascist government had offered for its violation of Ethiopian sovereignty. Pucci's book, Pratolini declared, "succeeds in presenting to us a documented picture of Ethiopia's barbarous, anarchic, medieval conditions, and of the necessity, the duty that impels Italy to undertake an integral and redemptive conquest in the physical and moral interest of the natives themselves."[7]

But there was another aspect of the Fascist movement which appealed to young Pratolini. In addition to hero worship, the mystique of violence and conquest, and the cults of youth and activism, he was also inspired by fascism's oft-proclaimed intention to build the kind of just social order which, he felt, could not be achieved by bourgeois liberalism, socialism, or communism. For Pratolini, as for so many of his contemporaries, fascism was the equivalent of state socialism, but a socialism with nerve and muscle. The ideal which inspired him was the utopian vision of a nation of workers and intellectuals bound together in indestructible unity. His allegiance to fascism was based in part on his belief that Mussolini's regime would "transcend" socialism and would resolve the grave economic and social problems that plagued Italy. He was convinced that fascism was essentially an equalitarian movement whose principal aims were the elimination of capitalism and the establishment of a just social order.

Following the victory in Africa, Pratolini praised the soldiers who had chosen to remain in Ethiopia to work the land. He reminded his readers that fascism, as an essentially equalitarian movement, must not allow speculators and capitalists to exploit the common men who had fought for their country. These men, he said, "must not fall under the burden of indigence or be led to believe that they are still working for a 'boss.' The state guarantees them these rights, and the state is the only employer that has a reason for being." [8] But fascism had not repudiated capitalism, and Pratolini began to have certain apprehensions about the direction in which the Italian government was moving after the Ethiopian campaign. The corporative economic system created by fascism had facilitated rather than impeded the profiteering of capitalist speculators, and Pratolini noted this fact in an article entitled "corporative industrialization," published in *Il Bargello*, September, 1936. Several months later, Pratolini reiterated, now with more hope than certainty, his belief that fascism would raise the intellectual and social level of the masses: "We think that it is perfectly orthodox to grant all men the right to perfect themselves; we believe that we have the obligation, as Fascists and revolutionaries, to give all Italians the possibility to achieve intellectual, social, and moral development." [9]

It was during the summer of 1936 that Pratolini met Elio Vittorini, who was among the first in Florentine intellectual circles to make a decisive break with fascism. Vittorini brought the fact of massive international protests against Franco's rebellion to Pratolini's attention and asked him how it was possible to reconcile fascism's claim of being a "people's" movement with its military support of the falangist armies in Spain. [10]

In September and October of 1936 Pratolini published two articles in *Il Bargello* which reflect the crisis of conscience he experienced following the conversations with Vittorini. Both deal with the Spanish Civil War, which had thrown him into a state of inner turmoil. In the first article he pointed out that Franco's rebellion was unworthy of Italy's support, since it was being led by "priests and generals whose doctrine was very bourgeois and very little proletarian." [11] In the second article, which appeared two weeks later, Pratolini noted that "the talk of social justice on the part of General Franco is a good sign, but we are unable to reconcile it with his former acts and with the speeches of Mola, Cabanellas, and Quiepo who, it would seem, intend to impose a real military oligarchy on the government and a triumphant revindication of capitalism and clericalism." [12] Thus, by the latter part of 1936, Pratolini had already taken a firm stand against militarism, capitalism, and clericalism, and had strongly identified himself with the working classes.

None of Pratolini's early political writings give any evidence of his having been introduced to Fascist ideology by a particular person or group. Fascism was so to speak "in the air," and Pratolini responded to the slogans and policies of the regime with the intense fervor that is often characteristic of youth. His writings on literary themes, on the other hand, almost always reflected the influence of other writers whose work he admired, and with whom he felt a close spiritual affinity.

Among Pratolini's first literary mentors, by far the most important was the Florentine painter Ottone Rosai. Pratolini met Rosai in 1931, at a time when he began to feel the need to read and study in a more systematic fashion than had been possible during his earlier adolescent years. Rosai introduced Pratolini to the poetry of the French symbolists and to the works of the Italian *crepuscolari*. It was under his guidance, also, that Pratolini first read the works of Giuseppe Ungaretti, who represented one of the most modern and experimental poetic voices in Italy. Pratolini's most significant reference to Rosai appeared in an article he wrote in defense of Rosai's artistic methods and aims. Rosai had been criticized for too often deriving the themes of his work from the life of the poor and the oppressed. Pratolini's defense of Rosai was based on his own conception of art as an instrument of moral edification. This notion that art must fulfill an educational function in society underlies the bulk of Pratolini's early literary and art criticism:

If art is spiritual teaching, betterment, a force that impels one to think, to believe, to perfect oneself (and what else is it but this?), then if he had allowed his world its vices and distortions, he would not have given his world the possibility of correcting itself, and he himself would have been crippled by it. Rosai avoided this danger when, in an artistic sense, he stopped feeling pity in order to be integrally human.[13]

During the early 1930's, of course, Pratolini's literary judgments often reflected the single-minded ardor of the Fascist zealot. For example, in July, 1932, he praised d'Annunzio for his "virile and combative career as writer and patriot," [14] and in February, 1933, he directed some scornful invective against a Florentine theatre company whose plays he characterized as "stuff that barely makes one smile because of its comic-stale plots, and that is in complete contrast to Fascist thought." [15]

By the mid 1930's, however, Pratolini had begun to shift his emphasis to questions of form and style. In his review [16] of Romano Bilenchi's novel *Il Capofabbrica*, published in the early months of 1935, Pratolini made a number of critical judgments which indicate that he was then moving away from a narrowly doctrinaire approach to literature. He admired in particular Bilenchi's stories of adolescence, which in his view were refreshingly free of bombast and ideological platitudes. In speaking of Bilenchi's style, Pratolini noted that "The word is intended as 'essentiality,'" without being the fruit of a cerebral or forced virtuosity; Bilenchi's language gives back to the word its representational function by virtue of its Tuscan purity (sana toscanità) which stems from the best tradition." It is difficult to define precisely what Pratolini meant in saying that Bilenchi's language "is intended as 'essentiality,' " but certainly this judgment must be viewed in terms of the impact that the poetry of Giuseppe Ungaretti had had on Pratolini's conception of language. The word "essentiality" refers to the qualities of purity and vibrant immediacy that Ungaretti had sought to achieve in his poetry. It conveys the idea of the poetic word whose value is not only symbolic or referential, but which is immediacy itself. It signifies the direct emotive impact of

words and images, that is, their unencumbered correspondence to the thoughts and feelings of the poet. The
reference to the "Tuscan purity" of Bilenchi's language
is also significant in that it indicates Pratolini's sensitive
appreciation of the stylistic elegance, clarity, and precision
which have distinguished Tuscan writers through the
ages.

Bilenchi was among Pratolini's closest literary and political associates in Florence. They were both ardent sup-
porters of fascism up to the outbreak of civil war in Spain,
when they began evaluating the slogans of the regime in
a new light. They also shared a strong if somewhat abstract
belief in literature as an instrument of social progress.
Bilenchi, however, had seen much earlier than Pratolini
that a one-sided emphasis on ideological dogma was possibly an effective weapon in political warfare, but that it
could only do injury to the writer. The writer's primary
function, Bilenchi thought, was to reveal the inner life of
his characters, not make them mouthpieces for political
doctrine.

Aside from certain of his immediate contemporaries
(Romano Bilenchi, Alessandro Parronchi, Berto Ricci, Elio
Vittorini), to whose works he was drawn by reason of the
common problems and aspirations he shared with them,
and the older, already established poets and novelists with
whom he felt a close affinity, such as Dino Campana, Ungaretti, and Fernando Agnoletti, a number of other writers
aroused young Pratolini's enthusiasm. The most important
are François Villon, Aldo Palazzeschi, and Federigo Tozzi.
"With Giuliotti," Pratolini wrote in September, 1936, "I
have in common two great and undying loves that perhaps
derive from opposed feelings: Tozzi and Villon." [17] Domenico Giuliotti, one of the Catholic writers of *Il Frontespizio*, had published a brief article on Villon in January,
1933. His definition of Villon as "a comic, macabre, erotic,
elegiac, and at time supremely religious man" [18] stimulated
Pratolini's curiosity about the French poet. But of even
more immediate interest to him was Giuliotti's statement
that Villon had derived artistic inspiration from "his own
passions and the passions of the men who surround him,
enclosed like him within the walls of the same city."
Though still uncertain as to the precise direction in which
he would move, Pratolini felt instinctively that he, too,

would one day return in his works to the experiences and passions of his youth, and that proletarian life in Santa Croce and San Frediano would provide him with some of the basic themes of his art. Thus when he read of the adventures, joys, and sorrows that Villon had experienced in a working-class quarter of fifteenth century Paris, he took the French poet to his heart.

Pratolini has always had deep respect for the art of Aldo Palazzeschi. In fact, as early as 1932 he singled out Palazzeschi and d'Annunzio as writers to whom the youth of Italy could turn for creative inspiration, and in many of his other critical writings in *Il Bargello* there are brief but significant indications of his unflagging interest in Palazzeschi's work. The sense of place, of intimate identification with the Florentine landscape that Palazzeschi manifested in his superb *Stampe dell'Ottocento* (1932) and in his novel *Le Sorelle Materassi* (1934) corresponded to Pratolini's reverential affection for his native city. But there was another aspect of Palazzeschi's work which Pratolini admired, namely his understanding of the sentiments and attitudes characteristic of the bourgeois milieu of which he was a part. He felt that Palazzeschi had succeeded in capturing the spirit of his age and in creating vivid character types, representative of a particular social class:

> Palazzeschi, as a complete artist and mature prose stylist, creates his world with absolute sincerity, . . . that is to say, he becomes the intimate chronicler of our times—for the purpose of establishing some parallels, Balzac, or better still, Flaubert, were in this sense chroniclers—Palazzeschi reveals to us the most hidden aspirations of men, the most intimate and secret facets of the human heart. He sheds light on feelings that men barely communicate to each other even while their actions suggest and favor the desire for such communication.[19]

Pratolini's enthusiastic response to the work of Federigo Tozzi stemmed from somewhat different motives than those which attracted him to Palazzeschi. In the early months of 1935 Paolo Cesarini published a short biography of Tozzi which Pratolini reviewed in *Il Bargello*. After indicating that Ottone Rosai had introduced him to Tozzi's work in 1931, and that he had read *Tre croci* and

Con gli occhi chiusi with a feeling of spontaneous pleasure, Pratolini said that he wanted his "comrades" to know
Tozzi for his "strength, humanity, and sincere patriotism."
Yet in explaining the basic reasons why he had found
Tozzi such a powerful and sincere writer, Pratolini suggests that personal rather than ideological motives had
drawn him to the Sienese novelist.

> And I who know Tozzi not through vague rumors but
> directly from his novels, which are of course all autobiog-
> raphies in the third person (Pietro, Dario, Virgilio, Re-
> migio, Enrico) that reflect his continual tragic suffering,
> sorrows, disappointments, and his "violent need for love,"
> I who was already in agreement with Cesarini's premise,
> after this brief presentation of Tozzi's life, feel an intensi-
> fication of the love and esteem that I have always had for
> him.[20]

It would be difficult to cite works which are more
fatalistic in conception and more pervaded with a sense of
defeat and disillusionment than Tozzi's *Tre croci* and
Podere. This was not the kind of brightly optimistic literature that could be used to inspire Fascist youth with confidence in a glorious future. But in his effort to reconcile
Fascist ideology with his instinctive predilection for writers (even the most pessimistic ones) whose emotional
sincerity precluded a one-sided emphasis on political
themes, Pratolini occasionally allowed incongruous juxta-
positions of ideas to obfuscate his genuine literary insights.
Thus he concluded his article on Tozzi by declaring that
Tozzi's writings of 1918 and 1919 were "the spiritual testimony of a Fascist of the time." There can be little doubt
that it was Tozzi's truthful descriptions of his own life
experiences, and not his late political manifestoes, which ac-
counted for the "love and esteem" that Pratolini felt
for him.

As indicated in the preceding discussion of Pratolini's
political and critical articles in *Il Bargello*, the years 1935
and 1936 marked the beginning of his disengagement from
fascism. This process of disengagement manifested itself
even more clearly in his writings in *Campo di Marte*. In
1938 and 1939, he was still involved in fascism, but no
longer as a partisan. He became an observer and a critic

and assumed the responsibility of bringing into focus some of the contradictions in Fascist culture which he felt competent to judge and to evaluate. It became immediately apparent in the first issue of *Campo di Marte* that Pratolini and Gatto had no intention of indulging in patriotic rhetoric. It was also clear that they had serious doubts about the perfection of the existing social order. After summoning all men of good will to collaborate in his attempt to create an honest, independent publication, Pratolini asserted his right to seek out the defects of the present in order to formulate new values for the future. He assured his readers that the editors of *Campo di Marte* were neither lackeys nor opportunists:

> As men of letters we shall not forget to trust in the intellect, as men we shall try to say something that is not a mere repetition of midnight chitchat. We are in nobody's employ . . . and we shall not defend any special interest groups.[21]

The tone as well as the content of Pratolini's writings in *Campo di Marte* is noteworthy. There is a dispassionate, reflective tone to these later writings which, in comparison with the hyperbolic stridency of many of his articles in *Il Bargello,* indicates a marked advance in his emotional and intellectual development. A characteristic feature of his writings in *Campo di Marte* is his frequent use of such words as "clarification," "revision," "discrimination," and "analysis." He was opposed, he said, to the "myth" of the Fascist colossus, and to the artificial systematization of doctrine which, he maintained, was incompatible with truly revolutionary thought:

> It seems to us that we are passing through a period that demands a revision of all our ideas, which are numerous and not always orthodox. We shall dedicate our work to a documentation of ourselves, to a more precise examination of that which our faith has caused us to believe. We shall make every effort to clarify our judgments of experiences and ideas belonging to our generation, and we shall deny our generation the right to chauvinism and internationalism, shallowness and pedantry.[22]

Pratolini's most interesting writings in *Campo di Marte*

are on literary themes, and it is in this area that his development manifests itself in a striking manner. As co-editor of a widely read literary review, he felt that it was his responsibility to initiate an objective inquiry into the actual literary products of the Fascist era, and to take stock of general trends in the arts during the preceding fifteen years.

By 1938, it had become impossible for Pratolini to praise third-rate novelists and poets solely because they apotheosized Mussolini or demonstrated their belief in Fascist ideology. He felt a moral obligation to defend the ideal of literature itself against the encroachments of propaganda, bombast, and sentimentality. In his review of Gian Paolo Callegari's novel *La terra e il sangue*, Pratolini expressed his opinion of the "Fascist novel":

> There is a place, on the margin of literary history, for a narrative (and for a poetry) of political propaganda.... However, the degeneration into which this literary genre has fallen today in Italy forces us to reflect on the unfortunate shallowness of the political faith that animates its practitioners and on the problematic competence of its critics.... Therefore, it is extremely important that we reach some agreement as to fundamental literary standards and qualities.
>
> The plethora of "prizes" on the basis of political considerations facilitates the improvisations of opportunists. We are presented with novels in which totally artificial, inhuman, and unimaginative motifs crowd in on the souls of the characters and the milieu in which they move. Thus we have men separated from feeling and normality, forced into making journalistic discourses of the most outworn conformism; discourses that are made in the service of a mythification, rhetorical beyond belief, of the earth, the hero, of Maternity and of the Nation. In addition, all of this is often expressed in a language that is pedestrian, ungrammatical, devoid of inventive resources, falsely mystical, and absurdly fatalistic. Examples [of this kind of writing], and they are not rare, are readily available as soon as a reader in good faith feels himself capable, in regard to those texts, of a calm examination of his own conscience.[23]

"The extreme orthodox," Pratolini said, "do not seem to realize that cultural chauvinism can only prevent the

Italian people from participating in a more creative literary civilization.[24] He argued that the consequences of a one-sided political orientation had been disastrous for literature, and suggested that while polemics and personal invective had their place in art, they were to be considered as means to an aesthetic end, not as ends in themselves.

In the one year of its existence, *Campo di Marte* performed an important function in Italian culture. The review brought many of the contradictions inherent in Fascist society to the attention of its readers, and attempted to make what Pratolini was later to call "a reasoned and responsible revision of ideas and principles."

II *The Poetry of the Commonplace*

With the exception of "Twenty Years in the Life of Uno," a short story which appeared in *Il Bargello* in March, 1935, none of the ten fictional works Pratolini produced during the 1930's would lead one to believe that he was struggling for the advancement of the masses, or that he had an ardent belief in the superior "revolutionary" morality of fascism. Instead one discovers that he was more interested in the evocative power of language, as reflected in the prose poems "Summer Fantasy" (1932) and "Episodes" (1932); in the theme of young love shattered by poverty and sickness, the central motif of the short stories "Story of a True Love" (1934) and "Gesuina" (1937); and finally in the themes of family life and personality development, as shown in the prose poems "1917" (1936), "The Hand" (1937), and "The Green Rug" (1937), and in the short stories "A Memorable Day" (1936) and "Early Childhood" (1938).

Pratolini's first two published works, short prose poems entitled "Summer Fantasy" [25] and "Episodes," [26] reveal his early interest in the evocative power of language. The opening of "Summer Fantasy" contains some vibrant, sensuous imagery coupled with a tribute to the healing power of the sun that are reminiscent of d'Annunzio:

> Recumbent on the earth burned by the ferocious diurnal heat—eternal and domestic fire—of the sun, I yearn to receive from its rays the certainty of being.

In "Episodes" Pratolini displays the same tendency as in "Summer Fantasy" to use a common, everyday experience as the point of departure for poetic creation. There is a fresh, lively sense of wonder expressed in this work which reflects not only the ebullience of youth, but also an instinctive responsiveness to the most ordinary aspects of life.

Very little can be said about the story "Twenty Years in the Life of Uno," [27] since most of it was rejected by the censors because of its "anticlerical" content and was never printed. Evidently, Pratolini had developed a fierce hostility not only to the church hierarchy, but also to Christian teachings, which he considered incompatible with the Fascist mystique of violence and conquest. The story describes the early experiences of a young man whose life had been conditioned by Fascist education, and who was in Pratolini's view a typical product of the new social order.

Two of Pratolini's early short stories, "Story of a True Love" [28] and "Gesuina," [29] deal with the theme of young love shattered by poverty and death. "Story of a True Love" takes places in an unnamed Tuscan country village and is noteworthy for its impressionistic, rhythmic language and the humble obscurity of its characters. At the beginning of this story, Pratolini describes the "pagan" love affair of Aldo and Rita, dwelling delightedly on their passionate caresses in the open fields at sunset. Then, the mood suddenly changes from one of serene joy to despair. Aldo leaves the village to become a *carabiniere*. He writes often to his beloved but receives no reply from her. Several years later he returns home, only to find that Rita has gone mad and has been put away in an insane asylum.

The girl portrayed in "Gesuina" bears a striking resemblance to the anemic, pathetic heroines of *Le amiche*, a series of autobiographical stories of young love, published in 1943. Gesuina feels an intense need for love and human warmth, but the squalid conditions in which she lives, and the long hours she spends each day working in a candy factory, have robbed her of her youth and hopes. She is only eighteen, but poverty has taken its inexorable toll:

> She was young, but she had always worked hard and eaten little; her face was already wrinkled, and her skin

was turning a yellowish color. It seemed that she had never taken a bit of sun. . . . She was a pitiable thing whose impoverishment was revealed even by a reflection of light or of the moon.

Of greater significance than the works just discussed is a group of five prose poems and short stories that Pratolini wrote during the second half of the 1930's. Despite his theoretical belief in the educational and social functions of art, these latter works ("1917," "The Hand," "The Green Rug," "Early Childhood," and "A Memorable Day") [30] show that young Pratolini actually viewed writing as a process of self-discovery, as a means to deepen his understanding of the people and experiences that had been of decisive importance in his early life.

"1917" is a short prose poem which describes a strange encounter between a four year old boy and his mother. For Pratolini this incident had symbolic undertones, since in a characteristically direct statement to the reader, he reveals that "my entire childhood is enclosed in that morning." In the first paragraph a brief allusion to the absence of the father, who is away at the front, immediately suggests an atmosphere of sorrow and tension and prepares us for the encounter which is to follow. The boy is ordered by his grandmother to go to his mother's room and to tell her that the midmorning snack of milk and cookies is ready. When she sees him, her face darkens. Tormented by fear that her husband will be killed in the war, she bitterly resents her son's boisterous intrusion into her privacy. The boy is frightened and bewildered, the mother inscrutably distant. At first, only her eyes register the conflicting feelings of hatred and pity tormenting her:

My mother was seated in front of the dressing table; her long black hair, which she was slowly caressing with her comb, her dress was white. I saw her from behind and her face met mine cruelly like the face of an archangel. Her eyes stared at me from the mirror, calm and wicked, astonished, green and black; her hand stopped moving; her gaze had frozen me at the entrance of the room, and for instants in which time ceased to exist, she stared into the mirror at me, with the burden of an invincible hatred, with the despair of one who has tried in vain to love even more intensely than is humanly possible. . . .

She threw the comb irritably on the dressing table, and her eyes darkened even more with hatred and pity:—He doesn't cry, my God, even he is unable to cry,—she said. (p. 8)

In "The Green Rug" Pratolini gives us a brief description of certain childhood experiences that had remained fixed in his mind. In the concluding paragraph, he focuses our attention on the fundamental facts of his early life. The words "dark," "poverty," and "relic" convey the predominantly melancholy mood of his childhood years:

I say that my mother had not died; it was she who taught me to read, under the six-cornered lamp, on the green quilted rug which my grandmother, in her extreme poverty, conserved like a relic. (p. 26)

The most noteworthy feature of "Early Childhood" is that it tells a story that unfolds in accordance with the requirements of narrative rather than prose-poetic writing. The causal nexus linking one incident to the other is not merely suggested or rendered in symbolic terms, as in "1917" and "The Green Rug," but explicitly stated and explained. Compare the beginning of "1917," for example:

If the image occurred in the life which we live, and my mother was still walking among men with her beauty and her destiny . . . (p. 3)

with the beginning of "Early Childhood":

When I was a child of four, it happened that my mother became pregnant a second time. My father was convalescing from wounds he had sustained in the war, and he felt far away from his woman; I learned later that he wrote her desperate letters imploring her to be near him. (p. 9)

The story "A Memorable Day" reveals an entirely different facet of Pratolini's personality. Whereas the charm of "1917" and "The Green Rug" derives from the poignant revocation of isolated moments in the past, the essential value of "A Memorable Day" lies in the dramatic and suspenseful unfolding of a narrative in which the objective world, and particularly the sense of place, begin to assume great importance. The word "place" must be emphasized, since in this story we encounter for the first time the names of streets and squares that will form the background of Pratolini's novels of Florentine life. "A Memorable Day" is, in the first place, a portrait of a "community" of rebellious, impoverished adolescent boys who live in the working-class quarter of Santa Croce. Pratolini's picaresque vagabonds have a shrewdness and resourcefulness which stand them in good stead in their war against established authority. They are outspokenly delinquents, but rarely calculating or malicious. The five boys portrayed in the story, Foffo, Rossini, Dino, Giordano, and Gino, along with the narrator himself, function as a tightly organized social unit with duties and privileges that are shared in common. Their greatest asset is loyalty, their principal virtue an indestructible sense of group solidarity. They belong to Florence's lumpen-proletariat:

> boys of twelve to sixteen years of age, the sons of workers and clerks, but more precisely of poor people who lived on miracles, itinerant salesmen, irresponsible idlers very often: children grew up alone there . . . , their fathers "with neither trade nor art," their mothers dishevelled at the front doors of the houses, in a poverty tinged with dignity, where everyone managed to eat with wine and a little extra, in that adjunct of San Frediano . . . which was the Quarter of Santa Croce in the Florence of 1921 . . . (p. 30)

Also worthy of note is the fact that "A Memorable Day" describes a series of facts, things, and persons closely observed and depicted with an almost naturalistic attention to color and detail. Interwoven into the story, which describes a day in the life of the "community" of boys, culminating in a savage street fight with a rival gang, are a series of psychological observations, character portraits, descriptions of Santa Croce, and several rather lengthy digressions in which Pratolini explains the meaning of slang words and phrases peculiar to the youngsters of his quarter. Thus, in addition to being a vivid account of a day in the lives of six Florentine boys, "A Memorable Day" also contains an abundance of information pertaining to the language and customs of a particular segment of Florentine society.

The character of the narrator himself also deserves

comment, for it is through an explanation of his own feelings and attitudes with respect to his boyhood companions that Pratolini elucidates the central theme of the story: the sense of solidarity that governs the relations between the six members of the "community." Before joining forces with Foffo and the others, he had both envied and feared them. Envy had prevented him from judging them objectively, while fear had compelled him to renounce his craving to commit himself to exploits that would test his moral and physical courage. Only after becoming a member of the community does he begin to evaluate each of the boys in individual terms and, consequently, to develop an awareness of his potential responsibilities to each separately and to the group as a whole.

> it seemed to me that only then did each of my friends acquire his true identity; I became aware of myself as one among other members of a mysterious society about which I must have dreamed very often, and in whose exploits I had delayed too long to participate. (p. 33)

"A Memorable Day" and the other autobiographical works indicate that by the latter half of the 1930's Pratolini had attained a high degree of technical competence. But of even greater importance is the fact that, in the words of Pietro Pancrazi, Pratolini discovered "in the poor, oppressed, and discordant world" of his childhood and adolescence "a rhythm, a sociality, a charm of its own." [31] The word "sociality" must be stressed, for it was through a depiction of his own early experiences within the context of family and community that Pratolini first discovered the significance of human solidarity and interdependence, values that were to form the basis of his conception of life in the years to come.

3 REMINISCENCE AND REMORSE
(1939–1943)

IN ADDITION TO his many scattered critical writings, book reviews, and prose poems which appeared in various periodicals,[1] Pratolini published four works between 1941 and 1943, which firmly established his reputation as a writer and critic. The first was *Il tappeto verde*,[2] an eighty-page volume of works written from 1936 to 1941 and considered by Pratolini as worthy of presentation to the broad reading public. The first two parts of this book contain the autobiographical vignettes of childhood ("1917," "The Hand," "The Green Rug," "Early Childhood") and the short story "A Memorable Day," which were discussed in the preceding chapter. The third part, which will be briefly examined in this chapter, comprises four prose poems, "On the Death of a Friend," "Itinerary of Memory," "Chicchirilla," and "Alibi," written in 1940 and 1941. All four of these latter works evoke a mood of sorrowful disenchantment and provide an accurate index of Pratolini's state of mind during the period now under study.

The second work, *Via de' Magazzini*,[3] is an autobiographical novella in which Pratolini returns to the themes of childhood and family life. It is largely a retelling of the events described in "1917" and "Early Childhood," but embraces a wider range of human feelings and experience than do the earlier works. The third is a critical edition [4] of Mario Pratesi's *L'Eredità* and *Le memorie del mio amico Tristano* which appeared in the fall of 1942. The fourth is *Le amiche*,[5] which was published in the summer of 1943. *Le amiche* is a collection of short stories whose principal motif is that of young love shattered by poverty and death. These stories are all "tales of poor lovers," but without the dimensions of hope and human solidarity that will characterize *Cronache di poveri amanti*.

Tullio Cicciarelli, the author of several laudatory reviews of Pratolini's autobiographical books, used the phrases "moral melancholy" and "spiritual exile" to describe the dominant psychological motifs of *Il tappeto verde*.[6] Indeed, these phrases not only characterize accurately Pratolini's own state of mind during the last years of the Fascist epoch, but also suggest the attitudes of pessimism and noninvolvement which prevailed in the Italian literary world following the outbreak of the Second World War.

Efforts on the part of Italian artists and intellectuals to make an objective appraisal of cultural and social problems within the framework of Fascist doctrine had met with failure. The fate of *Campo di Marte* is a case in point. Pratolini and Gatto had certainly not opposed the fundamental structure of the Fascist system. They had presented themselves as revisionists, not revolutionaries. Yet even the vaguest suggestion that Fascist society, as then constituted, did not represent the best of all possible worlds, or that the Fascist government had failed to realize its original political and economic goals, was judged by the official spokesmen for Fascist culture as heterodox if not subversive. An article published by Pratolini in the Roman literary review *La Ruota* in July, 1942, clearly reflects the painful situation in which so many Italian intellectuals found themselves during the latter years of the Fascist era:

> *Campo di Marte*—inadvertently prophetic of war in its name—was the last dispassionate attempt to initiate a dialectical exchange of views on a common and revolutionary level; an exchange which was designed to offer men of letters an opportunity to establish, within the new and eternal framework of a culture in movement, the essential values of poetry: poetry in verse, novels, and critical texts.
>
> I think that Gatto and I can affirm that we performed an act of faith in literature, welcoming and urging our friends to collaborate personally and autonomously in our enterprise. In the course of our work, and in the midst of

minor adversities which it is useless to report now, we were besieged by the blasphemous assaults of all those who in the name of the established order attacked us not with plausible reasons, but with vulgar invective and insults. Once again it was proved to us that instead of making a reasoned and responsible revision of ideas and principles, one had to register one's preference for the status quo.[7]

The advent of war did not bring about any fundamental change in the literary atmosphere that had prevailed in Italy during the preceding decade. New literary doctrines and manifestoes did not appear until late 1943, when the Resistance movement and Allied victories foreshadowed the ultimate collapse of the Nazi-Fascist regimes, and precipitated an intense ferment of literary and political activity. The outbreak of the war merely exacerbated tensions which had already been generated by political dictatorship, militarist propaganda, and the indiscriminate use of censorship on the part of the Fascist government. The difference between this period and the preceding decade was one of degree rather than of kind. The widespread disillusionment and rancor of the 1930's changed into the pessimism of the early 1940's.

Censorship precluded the free investigation of vast areas of life, so that in the late 1930's and early 1940's many writers, particularly of the generation to which Pratolini belonged, necessarily limited themselves to the description of personal feelings and experiences. One of the most characteristic features of the literary climate in Italy during this period was the appearance of many small volumes, both verse and prose, containing nostalgic reminiscences of childhood and early adolescence. Enrico Falqui noted this phenomenon when he said that, from 1938 to 1943, "writers of every region and condition were devoting themselves to the process of patiently unwinding the skein of their own youthful autobiographies in fragmentary writings."[8] In the opinion of Franco Calamandrei, the young writers of "the Fascist generation" fell back on "the only memory that their time offered them, the memory of tiny vicissitudes of childhood, of domestic mysteries and discoveries, of innocent affections and resentments."[9] Romano Bilenchi's *Anna e Bruno*, Libero Bigiaretti's *Care ombre*, Cesare Pavese's *Paesi tuoi*, Enrico Morovich's *Miracoli quotidiani*, Stefano Terra's *Rancore*, and of course Pratolini's *Via de' Magazzini* were among the many books published from 1939 to 1943 that were autobiographical in content and evoked the purity and trust of childhood.

Two closely interrelated patterns of thought predominate in Pratolini's writings during the period 1939 to 1943. The first is conditioned by the objective realities of the situation in which he found himself at that time and is composed of the motifs of solitude and estrangement. The second springs from his nostalgic return to the "lost paradise" of his childhood and adolescence.

The motifs of solitude and estrangement appear in various forms in the prose poems and lyrical fragments composed in 1940 and 1941. Each of the four prose poems that make up the concluding section of *Il tappeto verde*, "On the Death of a Friend," "Itinerary of Memory," "Chicchirilla," and "Alibi," give one the feeling that Pratolini was at that time bereft of almost all hope or consolation, and that he suffered intensely from loneliness and a persistent sense of guilt. "On the Death of a Friend" [10] is an elegiac tribute to a young Italo-American named Domenico Rotunno, who came to Florence in 1938 with the hope that a change of environment would cure him of the various mental and physical maladies that had plagued him in New York. Pratolini characterizes Domenico as a "man without a past" who lacked even the ability to "invent" a story for himself. In short, Rotunno was a defeated man with whom Pratolini shared a few hopes and many fears.

The city of Florence, which Pratolini will describe concretely and realistically in *Il Quartiere* and *Cronache di poveri amanti*, is in "Itinerary of Memory" [11] a chimerical, almost surrealistic landscape detached from any specific point of reference in time or place. "Chicchirilla" [12] was written in memory of a friend who had been killed in a naval battle in the latter part of 1940. Pratolini recalls a day he spent with his friend, a day of hiking and storytelling that had ended in a wooded area near Florence, where they had come upon a stray female goat. Chicchirilla proposed that they milk the goat, whose pitiful bleating did not then arouse the boys' compassion, but which now, in looking back on that day spent so happily with Chicchirilla, Pratolini treats as a symbol of sorrow and mourning. The central motif of "Alibi" [13] is human separateness, the inevitable sense of spiritual isolation that afflicts those for whom war, no matter how it is justified, is not a noble exploit, but rather the worst form of barbarism:

> I, and you, and you, and you,—we have become islands of ourselves. We have been compelled to possess a name to recognize each other, and each of us has had to sin to create a story for himself, to recognize himself in his sin, to say: this and this too is my sin. . . .
> But we are no longer able to know each other by name, now that something cruel submerges us, and it is the frightful cadence of jackboots. . . . We are filled with sorrow, poor creatures of God that we are. . . .

The other pattern of thought that predominates in Pratolini's writings during this period, a pattern of which *Via de' Magazzini* gives the fullest and most artistically resolved expression, is derived from his reverential attitude toward the emotions of childhood. The image of childhood and early adolescence as an age "in which all betrayals and all loves are still to be experienced" [14] exerted a powerful influence on Pratolini's conception of life. He had not forgotten "the nightmare of certain cold nights, after the death of my mother," [15] nor the terror he experienced as a boy whenever he thought of his mother, "so alone in her grave, so alone in the silence of the great cemetery." [16] But he also remembered the fresh sense of wonder, the discoveries, the ingenuous and intense enthusiasm that sustained him in childhood: "the days of the golden age, festive on the city streets open to the mystery of inimitable adventures . . . the water that I found fresh and miraculous at the fountain of San Niccolò." [17] Pratolini's art in *Via de' Magazzini* springs directly from this poignant contrast between one group of memories in which death and loneliness predominate, and another in which the image of childhood as a time of pure joy and discovery constitutes the principal leitmotif.

Since the feelings of solitude, remorse, and nostalgia

characterized Pratolini's state of mind during the period now under examination, it is not surprising to discover that his critical writings were rarely dispassionate appraisals of other authors, but rather that they most often reflected his own problems and aspirations. Three of these writings are worthy of attention: reviews of Piero Jahier's *Ragazzo* and of an anthology of Cesare Brandi's poems, and an introductory essay to the works of Mario Pratesi, a Tuscan "regionalist" writer of the nineteenth century.

Although Pratolini's review of *Ragazzo* [18] tells us nothing about the style or content of the book, which consists of prose-poetic reminiscences of a difficult and impoverished childhood, it does shed light on one of the motives which inspired him to write his own autobiographical books: Pratolini suggests that, for men who have achieved nothing of note in the world, the experiences of their own lives provide at once a justification for artistic creation and a reason for being: "Jahier has furnished us with the precise meaning of an autobiography that is the only justification for men without a past."

Pratolini's affinity with Jahier stemmed from the artistic intentions and spiritual feelings he shared with the Genoese writer. His enthusiastic response to Cesare Brandi's poems, on the other hand, was due not so much to any particular affinity he felt with Brandi himself as to the fact that he found in Brandi's poetry "an exemplary 'chorus' of motifs" that truthfully reflected the spirit of the time. Pratolini regarded Brandi as one of the "minor" yet eminently sincere "hermetic" poets.[19]

Of particular importance in Pratolini's introduction to Mario Pratesi's works is the distinction he makes between Pratesi's art and that of other nineteenth and twentieth century Tuscan writers such as Renato Fucini and Ferdinando Paolieri:

> I feel that in bringing Pratesi's *L'Eredità* and *Le memorie del mio amico Tristano* to the reader's attention, I am offering him texts that have the necessary qualities to stand the test of time and to earn for themselves a prominent position in Tuscan literature of the nineteenth century; texts, that is, which preserve and authenticate the typical linguistic and environmental characteristics of that litera-

ture which, unfortunately, has been reduced—by its famous latter-day imitators, from Fucini to Paolieri—to a decadent game of dialect and folklore. (p. 7)

In Pratolini's opinion, Fucini and Paolieri had limited themselves to a description of the external features of Tuscan provincial life and had contented themselves with delicate word paintings of the merely quaint and picturesque. In doing so, Pratolini felt that they betrayed the moral values which had inspired the best work of Italian regionalist writers. He believed that Pratesi, on the other hand, was worthy of being included in the distinguished group of Italian verists and regionalists who, in the latter part of the nineteenth and early twentieth centuries, created a body of literature rooted in the lives of the poor and the disinherited. Like Verga, De Roberto, Serao, Deledda, Capuana, and Di Giacomo, Pratesi brought a genuine passion for human equality and dignity to his writing. *Le memorie del mio amico Tristano* is a small book of childhood memories in which Pratesi abandoned himself to the bittersweetness of melancholy reflection. In his introduction to this work, Pratolini noted that "One senses in *Le memorie* an intimate, lyrical, and melancholy feeling; childhood is like a lost paradise whose purity the adult man fears he will offend as he prepares to evoke it in his art." (p. 12) Like Pratesi, Pratolini discovered in the experiences of his own early years a fertile source of narrative material. Both V*ia de' Magazzini* and *Le amiche* are, like Pratesi's *Le memorie*, pervaded by "an intimate, lyrical, and melancholy feeling," and reflect Pratolini's continued search for a meaningful context of human values within which to interpret and depict his own life experience.

V*ia de' Magazzini* was written over a period of four months in the latter part of 1941, and was published in March of 1942. Pratolini dedicated the book to the poet Allessandro Parronchi, who had been his close friend in Florence and fellow collaborator on *Campo di Marte*. In his preface to the second edition of V*ia de' Magazzini* (1949),[20] Pratolini speaks of the feelings and intentions that inspired him to write this work. He begins by describing a conversation in 1941 with the editor of a Roman newspaper which was publishing separate chapters of the book. The editor complained about the melancholy tone of his writing and suggested that he turn to happier thoughts. The editor's main point was that Pratolini's sorrowful evocation of childhood had nothing whatever to do with the content of the newspaper's front page:

> No, certainly, my pieces had no relationship with the first page of the Roman daily, but did they have any connection with the rest? With the men, that is, whom I vainly hoped I was reaching? (p. 8)

In view of his stated need to "reach" his readers, one might ask why Pratolini chose to remain within the narrow confines of the autobiographical novella instead of directly confronting the moral and political problems of the time. Pratolini continues by saying that it was not, as one might expect, the dictatorship or the fear of censorship that prevented him from exploring these problems, but rather a lack of capacity, an inability to speak for other men: "I was not able to speak for other men, to reveal their present sorrow. I avoided the obstacle and undertook to write of my private sorrow." (p. 8) He then explains that he became aware of his own identity during the period of the First World War, and that his memory of the "relationship war-sorrow-terror-solitude" which characterized his childhood had stimulated his need to write *Via de' Magazzini*. His principal purpose in this work was "to tell the 'story of a soul' who, after enduring humiliations and offenses, achieves liberation and love." Further on in his preface, Pratolini defines *Via de' Magazzini* as a "sentimental diary or, if you wish, the document, the chronicle, of a human condition." Although he hoped that the story of the person who says "I" in this book would "represent the story of all men who have had similar experiences," he did not pretend that he was writing about anyone except himself.

Although *Via de' Magazzini* is composed of a continuous flow of feelings, observations, and revelations expressed by the narrator, Valerio, and does not have the customary chapter headings, it can be divided, for the purpose of analysis, into four parts.

Part one sets the background of poverty and grave social

disorder against which the story of Valerio's life unfolds. The boy lives with his maternal grandparents and his mother, who is constantly tormented by fear that her husband will be killed in the war. The first part of the book culminates in the sickness of the mother, and ends with an evocation of the desolate loneliness that afflicts Valerio after her death. (pp. 13–33)

In part two, which opens during the weeks following the end of the war, Valerio experiences the emotional crisis whose impact and ultimate resolution represents the central psychological theme of the book. He withdraws into a totally unreal world in which he conjures up an image of maternal love and devotion that he had in reality never experienced. (pp. 34–42)

Part three begins with the return of Valerio's father. Three years pass, during which Valerio derives some solace from his father's friendly warmth. But once again his hopes are shattered when his father tells him that he intends to remarry. Then, the death of both grandparents, towards whom he had felt reverent affection, precipitates a second crisis in his emotional life, a crisis which is further exacerbated by the hatred he feels for his stepmother, Matilde. (pp. 43–70)

The concluding part of the book describes the boy's struggle for freedom and independence, and culminates in a precious moment of intimate communion shared by Valerio and his schoolmate Olga, who are drawn together by their mutual need for sympathy and compassionate understanding. (pp. 70–96)

Via de' Magazzini is, then, to a large extent an elaboration of essentially the same events and characters that Pratolini depicted earlier in "1917" and "Early Childhood." It differs from the earlier works, however, in two important respects. In the first place, Pratolini widens his angle of vision. The frame is enlarged to permit a more extended description of the atmosphere and general social background against which the story of Valerio and his family unfolds. Secondly, Pratolini explores in greater depth and detail the interdependent motifs of family life and personality development. The ambiguous relationship between mother and son, which was poignantly suggested in "1917," becomes the central psychological theme of

Via de' Magazzini. The suffering and humiliation endured by an impoverished Florentine family, briefly alluded to in "The Hand," represent in *Via de' Magazzini* aspects of a human condition which Pratolini renders in concrete, realistic terms. In "Early Childhood," Enrico's moments of crisis and illumination are revealed in expository statements directed to the reader, while the crucial experiences in Valerio's life are interwoven into the context of the narrative itself.

Pratolini describes the process of Valerio's development both in terms of his evolving attitudes toward himself and the members of his family, and in terms of his responses to the various people, places, and events that form part of the "outside world." The very first lines of the book introduce the motifs of discovery and dynamic movement which, in the course of the narrative, assume greater and greater importance in Valerio's life:

> I learned to distinguish one man from the other by looking through the spaces of a banister into a soldier's sleeping quarters. The school opposite my house had been transformed into a military barracks, and since the street was narrow—one of the medieval streets of Florence which in the center of the city form an island of silence—and the buildings seemed to bend towards each other as they ascended towards the sky, the third floors of my house and of the school became almost a single apartment.... From my observatory I saw a part of the room opposite me and in it soldiers came and went, sat on their cots, played cards, and spoke in strange dialects. (p. 13)

The child of five begins to observe and distinguish, and it is noteworthy that this process occurs first in relation to a group of soldiers rather than to the three persons, the mother and grandparents, with whom he is in daily contact. But the somber atmosphere of his home, his mother's constant melancholia, and his grandmother's rigid, stoical manner, weigh too heavily on the boy. The soldiers become his first friends, his first contact with the outside world. Then two years pass, and Valerio learns the meaning of privation and anxiety, of poverty and death. He sees that the suffering endured by his family is shared by all the poor people of Florence.

After his mother's death, Valerio turns to his grandparents, and particularly to his grandfather, in whom he
discovers qualities of mind and heart that he had not
previously experienced:

> What determined my affection for my grandfather was
> his respectful appreciation of my sense of wonder. . . .
> He shared my interests, discoveries, and disappointments,
> and from my point of view. (p. 31)

Valerio spends hours on end at his window that looks
out on the street, described repeatedly by Pratolini as an
"island of silence" amidst the noisy bustle of the city.
The rhythmic hammering of a shoemaker, the shouts of
street vendors, and the footsteps of occasional passersby
become symbols of hope to the boy. And it is precisely
his capacity to maintain a sense of hope amidst the static,
impoverished world in which he lives that proves ultimately to be Valerio's salvation, for he now experiences
the emotional crisis which will torment him for many
years. He finds a photograph of his mother when she
was a little girl, and immediately recognizes his resemblance to her:

> And suddenly, just as a room is illuminated or a train
> passes with an intense rush of wind, I became aware that
> that little girl resembled me. In her frown I recognized
> my stubbornness, in her clenched fist was enclosed my
> inability to express myself and to be understood. (p. 40)

Valerio also becomes aware at this time that men can
be cruel and violent. Thus far he has known only the
affectionate warmth of his father and grandfather, the
friendliness of the soldiers, and the reassuring sounds of
the shoemaker and street vendors on the street below.
But it is 1923, and the Fascists have set out on one of
their nightly punitive expeditions. Men of a different sort
present themselves to Valerio's consciousness in a bizarre
concatenation of screams and imprecations:

> Shrill screams resounded in the deserted square, "Rome,"
> said the screams, "is ours!" and the skull and crossbones
> undulated on the black flag, on the blackjacks that were
> being spun around above the heads in a tumult of oaths,
> of names being cheered. . . . (p. 59)

Following the second marriage of his father, and the death of both grandparents, nothing remains of his home on Via de' Magazzini except the memory of his mother. The family moves to Santa Croce, and there Valerio begins a new period in his life, "the desperate and unforgettable days of adolescence." He forms friendships with the ruggedly independent boys of his quarter, but the adventures he shares with his new comrades bring only temporary relief from the hatred he feels towards his stepmother with whom he argues and bickers constantly. At times, he longs to escape, to run off to some distant city and begin a whole new life. Nevertheless, though still oppressed by fear and loneliness, Valerio has become conscious of himself as an individual. He begins to acquire a sharper sense of his own dignity. Then his schoolmate Olga offers him love. Whenever he is in her presence, all his fears and hatred are dispelled:

> In her presence my turmoil was assuaged. I was at long last able to turn freely to another person; with her I discovered my ability to speak and to listen. (p. 92)

This is the simple "story of a soul" narrated in *Via de' Magazzini*, and certainly, when measured in relation to Pratolini's earlier prose poems and stories of childhood, it evidences a more dynamic conception of life, a deeper understanding of the interplay of internal and external forces that shape personality.

In contrast to the motifs of discovery, change, and development embodied in the story of Valerio's life from childhood to early adolescence, Pratolini depicts in *Via de' Magazzini* a "human condition" characterized by its sadness and immobility.

The central characters in this impoverished and static world are the mother and grandmother. What strikes one immediately is the contrast between the stubborn tenacity of the grandmother and the resigned fatalism of the mother. In almost every description of the mother, Pratolini suggests that she is a person who has lost the will to live, who looks upon death as a welcome refuge from the fears and anxieties that oppress her. The outstanding qualities of the grandmother, on the other hand, are stoicism and tenacity. An illiterate but natively intelligent woman, she devotes herself to the daily domestic chores of cooking, mending, and cleaning, all of which she performs competently and with tireless zeal. Valerio owes his life to the stubborn tenacity of his grandmother, for he had been a sickly child in need of constant care. Even after her daughter's death, she continues to work as diligently as ever to fulfill the responsibilities that give meaning and purpose to her life. When she becomes aware that age and hard work have taken their inexorable toll, she does not react with fear, but instead maintains her courage and will to live.

The characterization of the grandfather, referred to briefly in connection with the motifs of discovery and development, is especially noteworthy. Tender warmth radiates from this man who even in old age can still communicate his irrepressible zest for life. The grandfather is the only character in Via de' Magazzini whose background as well as present condition is described by Pratolini. The most significant element in his story is that he became, when still a young man, an ardent Socialist, and that he retained his Socialist convictions until he died in 1925:

> [He was] a liberal, and since he was a son of the people and a worker he was also an impassioned Socialist. Even in the last years of his life, old and undaunted, he read the "subversive" newspapers. (p. 30)

But the grandfather, too, despite his secret hope in the redemptive power of socialism, belongs essentially to the same unchanging "island of silence" as do the mother and grandmother. His joys and sorrows, his hopes and defeats, are symbolic of the "eternal occurrences in the lives of poor creatures" about which Valerio and his sweetheart Olga talk in the concluding episode of Via de' Magazzini.

Via de' Magazzini is in a number of important respects a key work in Pratolini's artistic development. The story of a boy's struggle for independence is placed within the context of a narrative that depicts the joys and sorrows of an entire family unit caught in the grip of poverty during the period of the First World War. The experiences of the various members of this family are in turn set against a more general social background. Valerio's development is portrayed fundamentally in terms of his growing awareness of the bond of solidarity and interdependence which links his life to that of his family and friends, and to the many other people with whom he comes into contact. These are motifs that Pratolini will continue to explore and develop in his future works.

Le amiche [21] contains seven short stories, written in 1941 and 1942, which describe the joys, but most often the sorrows, of young love; a few excerpts from the diary Pratolini kept at the tuberculosis sanitarium in 1935, entitled "Convalescent's Notebook," and two short autobiographical pieces, "My Father" and "The First Adventure."

Like Il tappeto verde and Via de' Magazzini, the stories in Le amiche are written in the first person. It is probable that most of them are drawn from life experience, yet in this case Pratolini's use of the first person appears very definitely to be a literary convention. All of the stories are constructed according to a set formula. Each begins with a series of nostalgic recollections of adolescence, and evokes the sights and sounds of Florentine life during the 1930's. These reminiscences are then followed by a description of a brief encounter between a boy and a girl. The girl is poor and lonely, while the boy, in a gallant but thoroughly naïve fashion, attempts to save her from the vices and cruelties of the world. For a moment, he is filled with hope. A kiss, an hour of intimacy, a passionate caress give him a sense of certainty. Then, his hopes are shattered. The idyl is interrupted and the river of life resumes its incessant flow. He is saved, but his sweetheart is caught in the whirling vortex and is lost to him forever. "Cora" and "Lida" do not follow exactly this formula, although the themes of defeat and disillusionment also appear in these stories. In neither of the two, however, does Pratolini present us with a sudden and tragic dénouement, as he does in "Jone," "Gloria," "Mara," "Bianca," and "Clara."

From a thematic point of view Le amiche must also be considered in relation to Pratolini's struggle, during the latter part of the 1930's, against the grotesque incongruities of the "Fascist novel." In view of his criticism of Fascist literature as being written "in the service of a mystification, rhetorical beyond belief, of the earth, the Hero, . . . and the Nation," [22] there can be little doubt that Le amiche represents an implied protest against the cult of the hero, and in particular against the mystique of violence and conquest. Pratolini's heroines are humble working girls, some of whom resort to petty deceits and prostitution to survive. Clara lives in a miserable hut near the river. Jone pretends she has a family, but in reality she is a lonely orphan. Bianca has a congenital nervous disorder. Gloria is a prostitute who dies of heart disease. Mara becomes the mistress of an unscrupulous business man. Cora is a poor, ignorant country girl. Lida spends her youth collecting money for a wandering guitar player.

Le amiche gives expression to Pratolini's reverence for love, and particularly for tender, adolescent love. In these brief encounters one senses the intensity and sincerity with which his adolescents reach out to each other. Pratolini's heroines are in their late teens, and are still pure in heart. The sordid conditions of their lives, and the compromises they make with the world, have not yet contaminated their souls. They are still capable of feeling genuine love, of performing a courageous act of faith, of offering a sincere compliment. It is their youth, their innocence and responsiveness to life that Pratolini exalts, and that he suggests will continue to flourish until the misery and corruption which surrounds them finally take their toll. Of particular interest is the singular purity even of "Gloria," a girl of nineteen who has been earning her living working in a brothel. The emotions which Pratolini attributes to her young lover are also worthy of note:

> As soon as we were alone, she became marvelous. For me it was sufficient that, instead of uttering a single other word, she said: "What a beautiful day it must be! Can you dance?" . . . I told myself that for the first time I was doing something for a woman, that for the first time a woman had complimented me on my hair and eyes, and not distractedly, as it had occurred to me to be complimented before, but in a genuinely altruistic manner. . . . I did not think about who she was, nor about what opinion she had of me, nor about what separated us in the eyes of the world. Nor did I even think about the fact that other men used her. It was enough for me that she was there, in her room between the bed and the dresser, with her gramophone. (pp. 226–28)

This same motif of inward purity that remains intact in

the midst of corruption appears in "Mara," who, despite her decision to begin working in a brothel, is still innocent enough to be proud of losing her virginity for love rather than money:

> She embraced me, with poignant intensity, she was warm and beautiful; she whispered into my ear: "Are you glad that I was intact?" (p. 240)

But in *Le amiche* love does not conquer all. In fact, so pathetic is the lot of these young girls that in most instances love gives way to pity and, unfortunately, pity often gives way in its turn to the rather banal sentimentality of the young man in each story who, for reasons of poverty, sickness, or death, is separated from his sweetheart.

In "My Father" Pratolini touches briefly on a theme which sheds further light on the meaning of these humble "tales of poor lovers" and on their place in Pratolini's artistic world. He tells us that, as an adolescent, he was sustained by a certain naïve egocentricity. He felt that the city belonged to him alone, and that everything had been created for his pleasure. But he soon learned that life demanded the acceptance of serious responsibilities, hard work and many sacrifices. He resolved to vindicate his father's suffering, but instead:

> it is the son who feels himself vindicated, who draws courage from the faith that his father has in him, who learns from his father's example that nothing else counts in this world except the strength to survive one's own destiny. (p. 195)

"The strength to survive one's own destiny"—a key phrase in the context of *Le amiche*, for it is precisely this "strength" which Pratolini's fragile heroines do not possess. They are among the many characters in Pratolini's short stories and novels who can be categorized as *vinti*, human beings who are defeated by evils with which they are unable to cope: poverty, sickness, loneliness, the cruelty or indifference of stronger individuals.

4 THE DISCOVERY
OF THE HUMAN COMMUNITY
(1943–1950)

THE RESISTANCE struggle, the revival of political freedom in Italy, and the postwar years of reconstruction coincided with an extraordinarily fruitful phase of Pratolini's artistic development. After *Le amiche*, Pratolini's artistic problem was no longer that of acquiring technical competence. It was, instead, to develop a new perspective, a new vision that would permit him to move beyond the restricted dimensions of the autobiographical novella, the short story, the delicate prose poem, the finely wrought *bella pagina*. It was Pratolini's participation in the Resistance movement that, more than any other event or experience, helped him to achieve this new perspective and determined the predominantly social character of his art in his major works of the period 1943 to 1950: *Il Quartiere, Cronaca familiare, Cronache di poveri amanti, Un eroe del nostro tempo*, and *Le ragazze di San Frediano*.

Pratolini's participation in the Resistance movement must be seen first against the background of its general characteristics. A basic characteristic of the Resistance movement in Italy was the universality of its ideals. The more than one hundred letters contained in the volume *Lettere di condannati a morte della resistenza italiana* testify to the fact that those who struggled in the Resistance were inspired above all by what one of the condemned patriots, Eusebio Giambone, called "the great and holy cause of the liberation of oppressed humanity." [1] Liberty and justice were the ideals that sustained Giambone and his comrades in their last hours of life.

The idea of political engagement, the conviction that cultural values could be saved only through concrete social and political action, represented one of the most important facets of the Resistance. Even while still engaged in struggle, certain of Italy's artists and intellectuals were already reflecting on the implications of their decision to join the Resistance. Giaime Pintor, for example, a gifted writer and critic of German literature who was killed while going from Naples to Rome to organize an underground in the Italian capital, in a letter to his brother shortly before his death wrote as follows:

> There comes a time when intellectuals must be capable of applying their experience to the common good, when each must be able to take his place in a fighting organization. . . . This is true above all in Italy. . . . Today in no civilized nation is there such a wide gap between potentialities and the conditions that actually prevail. It is up to us to bridge this gap and to declare the state of emergency. . . . Musicians and writers must forego their privileges in order to contribute to the liberation of all the people. . . . According to every probability, I shall be a mediocre partisan. Nevertheless it is the only possibility open to me and I accept it.[2]

Pintor sensed intuitively that the Resistance marked a decisive turning point in Italian history. His intuition has been confirmed by Italian political and literary historians, almost all of whom refer to the Resistance as an event comparable in its significance to the *Risorgimento*.

Pratolini's experiences as an anti-Fascist partisan began during the famous 45 days which intervened between the collapse of Mussolini's regime on July 25, 1943, and the signing of the armistice between Italy and the Allies on September 8.[3] During that period he traveled back and forth from Rome to Florence in an effort to establish contact with the leaders of the Resistance movement. He was more successful in Rome than in Florence, and in the latter part of September he decided to remain in the Italian capital. Pratolini carried on his work for the Resistance within the ranks of the newly reconstituted Communist Party. Working in close collaboration with the critic Franco Calamandrei and the writer Alfredo Orecchio, he wrote anti-Fascist propaganda, helped distribute clandestine copies of *L'Unità*, and presided over secret organizational meetings at various points in the sector under his jurisdiction. Pratolini's affiliation with the Communist Party was determined by a variety of motives. Like many other Italian intellectuals, he believed in 1943 that the Communist Party was the only party which had a revolutionary organization and program ready for action. He admired the Communists because they had been among the first to resist the rise of fascism. Many of the party's leaders, most notably Antonio Gramsci, had suffered imprisonment, exile and death for their beliefs. Another factor that influenced Pratolini was the courage and solidarity shown by the industrial workers of Piedmont, Lombardy, and Emilia throughout the years 1943 to 1945. Even under Nazi occupation Italian workers staged massive strikes protesting against Nazi methods and policies. These strikes were organized and led for the most part by Communists.

Though Pratolini's function in the Resistance was essentially political, from January to June, 1944, he also worked together with a group of men whose main assignment was the sabotaging of German tanks and trucks. In accordance with Rome's status as an "open city," the use of arms on the part of the citizenry was expressly proscribed. But since the Germans repeatedly violated an international agreement which forbade any army from moving troops or armaments into some sections of Rome, small groups of Resistance fighters, such as the one to which Pratolini belonged, felt justified in waging guerrilla warfare against them. Pratolini calls these men the "best and bravest of the people of Ponte Milvio." [4] In Ponte Milvio, Pratolini writes, "there existed the explicit solidarity of the poor and of those who wanted to become worthy of their own hearts." [5] Not once, in all his writings pertaining to the Resistance, does Pratolini make any reference to the influence that Marxist doctrine might have had on the Roman partisans. And, like the people of Ponte Milvio and Tor di Quinto, Pratolini's characters in *Il Quartiere* and *Cronache di poveri amanti* stand together not because they have learned about the value of working class solidarity from reading the *Communist Manifesto*, but because the very condition of their lives demands that they close ranks behind the barricades. But if, during this phase of his career, Pratolini associates the values of solidarity and interdependence with a "condition of life," he also concerns himself with ideas and commitments which cannot be explained solely in terms of the phrase "the solidarity of the poor." If this were not so, he would not have found it necessary to assign a specifically educative role to the Socialist Giorgio in *Il Quartiere*, to the Communist Maciste in *Cronache di poveri amanti*, and to the Communist partisans Bruna and Faliero in *Un eroe*.

Among Pratolini's closest friends in Rome was Vittorio Mallozzi, a kiln foreman who was captured by the Nazis in December, 1943, and executed, along with nine other Communists, on January 21, 1944. Because of his faith in the ideals of the Resistance, Mallozzi withstood the most dreadful torture, and never revealed any information to the Germans that might have jeopardized the safety of his comrades:

> My dearest comrade—he who had coordinated activities in our sector and given a discipline to our enthusiasm, and even to our ideological discussions—was arrested in December. He held the fates of all of us in his hands, he was familiar with our lives and miracles (and with our weaknesses too)....But none of us thought of looking for a different hideout, or of carrying our weapons to some other place....After he was captured, his words came back to us and seemed clearer and more indisputable than ever.... A month passed. It was the 21st of January. I was walking with another comrade. We both bought newspapers at a local newsstand and immediately our attention was attracted by a black line on the first page, beneath which there was a list of ten men who had been executed by a German firing squad. Vittorio Mallozzi was the third name on the list.[6]

It is probable that Mallozzi and other men of his calibre recalled to Pratolini's mind the faith and sacrifices of men he had known in his youth, since it is precisely the capacity to act on their convictions, to risk even death for their ideals, that is the distinguishing characteristic of Giorgio, Maciste, and Faliero.

The Resistance contributed directly to the revival of literary realism in Italy, a realism characterized by a strong interest in the theme of political conflict and in the struggles of Italy's proletarian masses. Since Pratolini was much influenced by the ferment of ideas that accompanied the restoration of freedom in Italy and has been called one of the chief exponents of literary neo-realism, it will be useful to indicate certain of the new realism's salient characteristics. The term "neo-realism" was first applied to certain postwar Italian films in which the grim facts of war, poverty and social disorder were often documented with considerable power. Almost immediately the term began to be applied to other art forms as well, most notably to literature. With specific regard to the postwar Italian novel, the term neo-realism was used for two reasons: to suggest a widespread postwar reaction against the purism and gentility of the art prose that had flourished during the preceding two decades, and to indicate that there existed a venerable tradition of realism in Italian literature from which the new novelists derived much of their inspiration, if not their actual themes.

All the writers and critics who replied to Carlo Bo's *Inchiesta sul neorealismo* in 1950 agreed with one of his premises, which was that neo-realism could not be called a "school." It was not a school, they felt, since it had no acknowledged leader, and had never promulgated a manifesto or doctrine. Most agreed with Niccolò Gallo, who called neo-realism an attitude of mind, a prevalent *stato d'animo*,[7] and with Sergio Solmi, who believed that novelists as different in temperament and vision as Pratolini, Brancati, Vittorini, Piovene, Calvino, Moravia, and others generally referred to as neo-realists could not possibly be grouped under a single category, even if they shared a common interest in political and social themes.[8]

What, then, *was* neo-realism? Was there any justification for speaking not of a school, but of a current, a trend in the postwar novel? The answers to this question were generally affirmative, and can be briefly summarized as follows: neo-realism, in its broadest sense, involved, in the first place, an implicit belief in an objective reality existing outside the writer. In the words of Alberto Moravia, 'neo-realism has postulated a new interest in an objective and factual reality and consequently the necessity to study and understand."[9] Secondly, neo-realism views the individual in relation to the society to which he belongs, and therefore documents the interrelationship between private motives and socio-political events. Thirdly, neo-realism implies a rejection of flowery and rhetorical language in favor of understatement, concreteness, and simplicity.[10]

If we are to judge from the documents available to us, it was the cinematographic rather than the literary side of neo-realism that had the most direct influence on Pratolini. In fact, Pratolini tells us that it was Roberto Rossellini who in February, 1946, urged and persuaded him to begin working on *Cronache*, and that the filming of the movie *Paisà* in Naples inspired him to return with his memory to the slums of Florence, to via del Corno, where he had lived as a boy:

> For two months I remained idle during that mild Neapolitan winter, in the midst of political fist fights and meetings; for the first time, a man of thirty, I was both a spectator of and participant in the political passions of the people. My dialogue with my dead brother had in a sense liberated me from every literary vice; to take pen in hand, to "organize" a story, to mystify feelings would have seemed to me both a puerile and an obscene exercise, comparable to filling page after page with curses. But then Roberto Rossellini came and awoke me from my sorrowful reverie, with his filming of *Paisà*, the troop of actors, Massimo Mida, my dear friend. He forced me back into life, to the tabarin of the Hotel Miramare, to the Amalfi coast, to the noisy squares of Naples as I followed his camera. Rossellini urged me to begin working on *Cronache*. The writing of this book was for me an indirect yet violent way of returning to the streets of my city, of savoring again its air, the color of its stones, the warmth of its people. I felt, then, that there exists another dimension in the creation of art, and it is that of making oneself the interpreter of the feelings of others—which is not mystification, but a more concrete truth, just as every gesture that transcends our private world of affections and exaltations, that turns to the understanding and unites itself with the protest of the collective, is more concrete and true.[11]

An examination of Pratolini's other literary sources and affinities during the period under study reveals that he

derived much inspiration from the early Florentine chroniclers and storytellers. Pratolini's interpretation of Florentine proletarian life in *Il Quartiere, Cronache,* and *Le
ragazze* is based on a general assumption about the totality
of Florentine history: that Dino Compagni would have
written essentially the same chronicle had he been born
in 1900 rather than 1260. In Pratolini's opinion, only the
names, not the personality traits, of Compagni's characters
would be different, as he said explicitly in an article written
in January, 1949:

> Florence is an ancient network of streets that resists all
> the onslaughts of weather and conflict, a sky in which
> vernacular and poetry thrive on each other and achieve,
> unwittingly, their immortality. That house with the slant-
> ing roof, on the square where the vegetables are sold, was,
> exactly as it appears today, the house of Cellini . . . ; and
> further to the right, after you have turned the corner, that
> window looks out from the house in which the author of
> Pinocchio was born and died, and in which he wrote his
> masterpiece; *we are what we are, Florentine history from
> 1919 to 1945 was written by Dino Compagni 600 years
> ago* (italics mine).[12]

The Resistance and the revival of freedom in Italy restored
Pratolini's confidence in man's capacity to change and to
shape his own destiny. Hence the idea of political engagement plays an important part in his novels. Yet para-
doxically there are numerous passages and situations in his
works which indicate that his conception of life was conditioned in large measure by his feeling that "Florentine
history from 1919 to 1945 was written by Dino Compagni
600 years ago." In fact, the meaning that Pratolini attributes to the word *cronaca* derives largely from his reading
of Donato Velluti, Giovanni Villani, and particularly
of Dino Compagni, with whom of the early fourteenth
century Florentine chroniclers he felt the closest affinity.
Pratolini's *Cronache* is a description of Florentine life
during the mid 1920's that in many respects parallels the
events and characters described in Compagni's *Cronica*.
Like Compagni, Pratolini writes of a period in Florentine
history in which "men who feared their adversaries hid
themselves in the homes of their friends: one enemy

offended the other ... men were killed"; of a Florence dominated by a regime under which "evil is not punished by law but since the evil-doer has friends, and can spend money, he is absolved of his wicked deeds." [13]

Among the writers of the nineteenth and twentieth centuries who exerted a direct influence on Pratolini, the most important are Victor Hugo, Charles Louis Philippe, Giovanni Verga, Mikhail Lermontov, and Alberto Moravia: [14] a heterogeneous group of writers to whom he was attracted for a variety of personal and literary motives. In an introductory essay to his translation of Hugo's *Choses Vues*,[15] Pratolini explained Hugo's position in nineteenth century French letters and discussed certain political and social events which influenced the themes of his major works. Some of the general comments Pratolini makes with respect to Hugo's art are strongly derogatory. For example, he maintains that the bulk of Hugo's work was "spoiled and corrupted" by the demands of "social pedagogy," and that the French novelist's inordinate egotism prevented him from dealing with the problems of his time in a spirit of fairness and objectivity. Yet with specific regard to *Choses Vues*, Pratolini writes with genuine enthusiasm. There can be little doubt that Pratolini's admiration for this little known work stemmed from the fact that he found in it the kind of truthful description of "the small and great secrets" of daily life which he himself would attempt to achieve in his own works, particularly in *Il Quartiere* and *Cronache*.

In his review of *Il Quartiere*,[16] the poet Eugenio Montale cited Charles Louis Philippe as a probable influence on Pratolini. Indeed, there is abundant evidence of the very close affinity that Pratolini felt with this representative of late French naturalism. Shortly before writing *Il Quartiere*, Pratolini translated Philippe's *Bubu de Montparnasse*,[17] and in 1945 he translated another of Philippe's novels, *Le Père Perdrix*, which, however, was never published. *Bubu de Montparnasse* is a novel set in Paris which describes the daily experiences of people who move in the same proletarian milieu as do Pratolini's adolescents in *Il Quartiere*. Like the inhabitants of Pratolini's Santa Croce, Philippe's characters, with their humble joys and sorrows, their instinctive sense of communal solidarity, and innocent candor, live in a world far removed from the surrounding metropolis. Philippe's Montparnasse stands in the same relation to Paris as Pratolini's Santa Croce does to Florence. Both are islands of proletarian humanity separated from the main stream of life by centuries of mistrust and the feeling of proud self-sufficiency.

From what has been said thus far concerning Pratolini's attachment to the poorest sections of Florence, his penchant for depicting the ordinary occurrences of daily life, and his deep interest in the themes of solidarity and human interdependence, it becomes clear why Giovanni Verga's short stories and novels, particularly *I Malavoglia*, struck a responsive chord in him. Pratolini's extensive use of the choral technique in both *Il Quartiere* and *Cronache* undoubtedly stems from his reading of Verga, for this technique corresponded to a mode of unanimistic feeling he shared with and perhaps even derived from the Sicilian novelist. It can be said also that although Pratolini infuses a more hopeful spirit into his stories of the Florentine poor, a hope which springs from his belief (that Verga did not have) in the redemptive power of love, many of his characters succumb to the same iron laws of poverty and loneliness as do Verga's *vinti*.

Pratolini wrote *Il Quartiere* [18] from September, 1943, to March, 1944. The novel was published in December, 1944, by *La Nuova Biblioteca*, whose purpose was, as stated on the book jacket, "to provide the people with writings that speak of the people, that portray the people in its struggles and labors, that reflect its life and reality." Pratolini dedicated the novel to

> the memory of my comrades and friends Giorgio Labò, architect, Vittorio Mallozzi, kilnman, Giaime Pintor, writer, Bruno Becchi, painter, who fell in the partisan war for freedom.

In *Il Quartiere*, Pratolini recreates the life of a Florentine working-class quarter, Santa Croce, during the years 1932 to 1937. Like *Via de' Magazzini* and the stories in *Le amiche*, *Il Quartiere* is written in the first person. In this work, however, the pronoun "we" is of far greater importance than "I." Valerio, the narrator, is one of a group of youngsters whose collective identity and struggle represents the pivotal point around which the action of the story turns. His own problems and conflicts are no more important than those of Carlo, Giorgio, Marisa, Olga, and the other members of the "community" to which he belongs.

In Chapters two through six, Pratolini introduces all the important characters of the novel and touches briefly on their family backgrounds, their dominant personality traits, and their relationships to each other. The personalities of the four principal male characters, Giorgio, Valerio, Carlo, and Gino, are briefly yet precisely sketched at the outset of the novel. Giorgio is the most earnest and mature. At the age of sixteen he is already fully conscious of his responsibilities, and from the very beginning of the story he plays the role of political and moral mentor. Valerio is the most advanced intellectually, but he is still very much the adolescent: alternately shy and expansive, painfully aware of the gap between his present capacities and his ambitions, and frequently assailed by intense sexual cravings which he yearns yet fears to satisfy. Carlo is even more full of contradictions than Valerio. At times he is inexplicably cruel and malicious and his moods change constantly, oscillating between the extremes of cordial jocularity and sullen aloofness. Gino differs radically from the other three boys who, notwithstanding their problems and fears, are capable of communicating their feelings to each other and, through communication, achieving that sense of warmth and communal solidarity which Pratolini denominates from time to time *il sentimento di Quartiere*. Gino is cynical, indolent, and resentful. He ridicules his friends' belief in the virtues of communal solidarity, calling it narrow-minded provincialism.

The personalities of the three principal female characters, Olga, Maria, and Marisa, are less sharply individualized. Olga is only fourteen when the story begins and is the most naïve and innocent of the three. Maria, who becomes Giorgio's wife, is at the beginning of the novel dangerously close to becoming a prostitute. Without parental guidance (her mother is ill with heart disease, her father was murdered in a tavern brawl), she allows herself to be "kept" by a man who promises her clothes and luxury. But Giorgio's steadfast faith in her and offer of marriage save her from the fate of a *donna mantenuta*.

Marisa is the most passionate and honest, and, therefore, the most vulnerable.

In the second part of the novel, Pratolini shifts back and forth from past to present in describing the life patterns and gradual development of his characters during the years 1933 to 1935. These are the crucial years of transition for the entire community of youngsters, for each now becomes involved in basic problems of love and identity.

The third and concluding part of the novel opens in September, 1935. Rumors of an impending war in Africa are circulating throughout the quarter. In January, 1936, Giorgio and Carlo are drafted. Giorgio spends a year in service in Italy and returns to his wife and baby boy in the early months of 1937. Carlo is among the first to be sent to Africa and is killed in one of the initial battles. Valerio, who is a year younger than Giorgio and Carlo, is not drafted until the latter months of 1936. He falls in love with Olga, and for a time it appears that they will marry. But Olga is still a child under the influence of her mother, who takes her away to Milan. Gino, utterly corrupted by a parasitic existence, is apprehended by the police in Rome and accused of the murder of one of his former homosexual benefactors. He admits his guilt, and in a long letter which he sends to his friends from prison explains, with remarkable lucidity, the events and experiences that led him to commit the crime.

In the last three chapters, Pratolini brings the various stories to their conclusions, principally by means of a series of letters which Valerio, now in service, receives from Giorgio, from his father, from Marisa, and from Arrigo, Maria's brother. In the final scene, Valerio returns to Santa Croce and visits Marisa. Together they walk through the streets of their quarter. Marisa asks him whether he thinks Carlo and so many other young men have died in vain in Africa. Valerio replies, "they have not died for nothing. . . . From their example we will learn to struggle so that we will not be betrayed again." (p. 220)

Il Quartiere ends, therefore, on a note of hope and affirmation. It is clear that Valerio, in his final symbolic role as spokesman for the people of Santa Croce, has undergone a change in attitude toward himself and, implicitly, toward the world in which he lives: prior to the war in Africa, he had been concerned exclusively with his own personal problems and aspirations. The fact that Marisa has developed the capacity to ask a basic question which affects not only her own future but the future of her community is also symptomatic of her transition from adolescence to maturity. Carlo, too, before meeting his death in Africa, acquires an understanding of the causes and potentially dangerous consequences of his vindictiveness. Giorgio does not change in any fundamental way, since at the beginning of the novel he displays the same qualities of earnestness and sincerity which distinguish his behavior at the end. On the other hand, in view of the fact that the principles of equality and solidarity about which he speaks in 1932 lead him, in 1936, to active resistance against the regime, it can be said that he also develops from an idealistic adolescent into a mature and committed man. Maria finds happiness as the wife of Giorgio and puts her adolescent yearnings for a life of unearned luxury behind her. Even Olga, despite her lack of independent spirit, which forces her to remain tied to her mother, acquires the courage to admit to Valerio that she is unworthy of his love. Gino, then, is the only character in *Il Quartiere* who fails to change and mature.

The reason for Gino's failure is closely interrelated with a theme that lies at the vital center of the novel: throughout the course of the narrative, Pratolini stresses the sense of solidarity that animates the community of impoverished adolescents in Santa Croce. In fact, the entire quarter functions as an autonomous "island" of proletarian men and women attached to each other by "private rancors" and "private loyalties." One senses the presence of a collective soul in this historic quarter, a sort of atavistic and indestructible spiritual impulse that courses through the blood of each individual and binds him to his community. The other quarters and areas of Florence seem to the people of Santa Croce to be somehow lacking in warmth and friendliness:

> It was after six o'clock when we finished work, and life and friendship and warmth had no existence for us until we were back home in our streets and squares. (p. 3)

The hope which sustains Valerio after his return from military service derives essentially from his faith in the enduring value of his relationships with Giorgio, Carlo, and the others. It is by virtue of their friendship and sense of collective identity that Pratolini's characters eventually acquire an awareness of their dignity as individuals. Interdependence nourishes independence of mind and spirit.

The tragic fate of Gino is ascribed by Pratolini in large measure to his loss of spiritual and physical contact with his friends. Because of the debilitating shocks he experiences during childhood, Gino becomes precociously cynical and suspicious and is unable to communicate his feelings to others. In Pratolini's view, Gino's fate was sealed as soon as he separated himself from his friends:

> He passes his hand over his lips and murmurs something about the world not ending at Porta alla Croce. And in so saying he is a traitor to the one true link that bound him to his friends: the sentiment of the Quarter and that power to face life and mold it with the strength of our bodies, shoulder to shoulder. (p. 72)

But Pratolini does not allow us to reach the relatively comfortable conclusion that Gino's perversion and crime are attributable solely to his neurotic incapacity for friendship. When Gino's friends learn that he has been apprehended by the police in Rome, and that he has confessed to robbery and murder, they feel compelled to share his guilt. Giorgio has the courage to express what is in all their hearts, when he affirms his belief in the principles of interdependence and collective responsibility.

From what has been said thus far concerning the way in which Pratolini describes his characters, it becomes clear that their "sentimento di Quartiere" represents at once the premise and the limit of their conception of life. Their emotional attachments to each other are conditioned by this "sentimento," as are their political and social attitudes. The novel opens with the statement that "we were happy in our Quarter," and ends with Valerio's determination to remain in Santa Croce, where "even the air and the sun must be defended behind the barricades." (p. 221) The premise and conclusion of Il Quartiere are virtually identical. Certainly the verb "defend" suggests a more dynamic view of life than the adjective "happy," and, as already noted, all of Pratolini's characters, with the exception of Gino, do undoubtedly develop and mature. But the vantage point from which Pratolini views the lives and destinies of his characters is the same at the end of the novel as at the beginning. The reasons for this paradoxical contradiction in *Il Quartiere* between the elements of dynamism and stasis, of progression and immobility, lie in certain of the implicit assumptions that Pratolini makes about his characters, and about the general process of life in Santa Croce.

It is difficult to reconcile one of Pratolini's main intentions, which was to describe the transition from adolescence to maturity, with the extraordinary "naturalness" and "simplicity" of his characters. Education is not a "simple" or "natural" unfolding, yet Pratolini uses these words constantly to characterize the thoughts and feelings of his adolescents. Everything in *Il Quartiere*, including political and social attitudes, is ultimately reduced by Pratolini to a question of "nature" and "instinct." The relationships between the boys and girls of Santa Croce are always explained by Pratolini in terms of "instinctive," "natural," or "spontaneous" feelings. For example, the attraction between Giorgio and Maria is compared, in a characteristic simile taken from the world of nature, to "the budding of a geranium at the window":

> Their love was consummated spontaneously one Sunday in September when they were left alone in the house. It was something simple and inevitable, like the budding of a geranium at the window, like the quiet flow of the Arno down to the sea. (p. 81)

Even the profound sense of human solidarity which animates the adolescents of Santa Croce, their loyalty and friendship, forms part of the "natural" rhythm and flow of life, and is compared, as always, to "simple" and "eternal" things:

> our feelings are simple and eternal like bread, like water that gushes from a fountain and slakes our thirst without our even noticing its taste. (p. 91)

The comparisons of human emotions with various natural

phenomena, which abound throughout the novel, and the extraordinary simplicity and spontaneity of these impoverished adolescents, are factors that contrast with, indeed virtually obscure, the underlying process of growth and development that Pratolini sought to describe in *Il Quartiere*.

As for the political theme proper, the conflict between fascism and anti-fascism, it must be said that Pratolini deals with it in the most hesitant and allusive manner possible. The fundamental naïveté and uncertainty of his characters explains their confused groping for values, yet in their groping Pratolini's characters do not even begin to reflect on ideological issues.

There is abundant evidence in *Il Quartiere* of the fact that Pratolini's imagination was stirred most intensely by a vision of the unchanging, "eternal" aspects of life in his quarter. The really key words in his description of life in Santa Croce are therefore not change and development, but rather "ancient" and "eternal." Pratolini's sense of the past is, of course, primarily that of a Florentine, as evidenced in the numerous parallels he draws between the citizens of Santa Croce in the twentieth century and their forebears in past ages:

> We are a people worn out from servitude and struggle; we pay the penalty for wrongs done centuries ago, our own wrongs, just as the faces that look down from Masaccio's frescoes in the Church of the Carmine are our own faces. (p. 91)

Pratolini's love scenes, always written with tender restraint and finesse, form part of the essentially immobile and immutable world depicted in *Il Quartiere*. Marisa reveals herself to her young lover Valerio with a completely unsophisticated naturalness that is characteristic of Pratolini's adolescents. Like so many of the episodes in the novel, this love scene seems to be the enactment of an ancient ritual, performed in an atmosphere of almost religious solemnity:

> The sun had gone down. With the first shadows of the evening the little cypress tress seemed to grow taller, rising up from the grass that bent to the cold wind. Marisa

and I were alone in the green silence. Her words asked too much of me, begged for a charity that my still adolescent heart was incapable of giving. The things she had told me were ancient truths, enduring like an echo from the past, a memory of ancient tyrannies and vendettas. Where the blame lay was of no importance. Her voice was clear and without anger as she told her story, a story that had been repeated from the beginning of the world until it had become a humble, everyday fact and nothing could alter it. Her words seemed to plead for help, not from me or from within herself, or from anything in this world—to plead for something that could put things right with a simple gesture, or a whisper, or the tolling of a bell in the evening air. (pp. 58–59)

Il Quartiere is a novel explicitly social in character, yet tender lyricism corresponds much more directly to its mood than a powerfully sustained, objective prose. It is not change which stirs Pratolini's imagination but rather the same "eternal occurrences in the lives of poor creatures" about which Valerio and Olga spoke in the concluding scene of *Via de' Magazzini*.

An essential characteristic of Pratolini's writing in *Il Quartiere* is a descriptive technique used at frequent intervals to convey the totality of life in his quarter. The "sentimento di Quartiere" shared by Giorgio, Valerio, Marisa, and the others constitutes the *animus* of the book, the spiritual basis for hope and commitment. The unanimistic spirit which pervades the novel is, therefore, appropriately conveyed in "street scenes" and in collective portraits of life in Santa Croce. These passages have a quality of immediacy and concreteness which show clearly that Pratolini is on terms of intimate familiarity with this "island" of proletarian humanity, and understands its life and rhythm, its misery and its dignity:

In springtime the geraniums blossom on our windowsills. Our sisters put them in their hair. Gaily they beat the blankets before storing them away in the bottom of the wardrobe, together with overcoats darned at the elbow and turned at the collar.

From one window to another, from one street to another in our Quarter goes the refrain of a song, taken up by a hundred voices and interrupted by conversation and shouts from inside the houses, where the breath of spring moves with its perfume of leaves and new-mown hay.

> The weary highwayman
> On milk-white steed
> Descends the mysterious Sierra
> And plucks the flaming rose . . .

says the song. Our dialect takes on an ancient purity; the voices which diffuse it from room to room, from alley to alley, have a new note of affection, as from lips whose thirst has been quenched at a spring sparkling in the translucent light of early morning, when the façades of our houses take on an air of dignity amid the squalor of peeling stucco and rusty drainpipes. . . .

Our Quarter is awake and humming with life and movement. Even the windows of the whorehouse in Via Rosa have been opened slightly from within, and the girls peep out curiously through the shutters. They wear pink negligees and have a ready laugh for the young blacksmith who holds the horse's hoof tightly between his knees as he doffs his cap. And our mothers empty out their purses on the table. Wrapped in their shawls, they do sums on their fingers before going out shopping. . . . (pp. 66–68)

Pratolini is not a detached observer of life in Santa Croce, but rather a participant and partisan. He writes from within his world. Therein lie some of the strengths and limits of *Il Quartiere*.

Cronaca familiare,[19] written in six nights during the latter part of December, 1945, is the life story of Pratolini's brother, Ferruccio, who died in July, 1945, at the age of twenty-seven. In a brief preface to *Cronaca familiare*, Pratolini explains that this book is not a work of fantasy, but simply an intimate dialogue between himself and his dead brother. His intention was to seek consolation, and also to offer these pages as a "sterile expiation" for his failure to recognize the spiritual needs of his brother until it was too late to help him.

The theme of emotional deprivation, of bitter and unrelieved loneliness, permeates the book. In the opening chapters we begin to understand Ferruccio's dilemma.[20] He is raised in an overprotected, sterile atmosphere in which the rules of hygiene are rigidly observed at the expense of freedom. He is pampered, fondled, doted on until his instinct for adventure and independence is almost completely obliterated. While Vasco plunges into a life of work and study, Ferruccio remains in the custody of the major-domo, who continues to treat the now adolescent boy as if he were still an infant in need of constant care.

Years later, Ferruccio, in his mid-twenties, is unable to cope with the daily problems of life. His marriage fails, he drifts from job to job, and his health declines. After the death of his protector, Ferruccio is compelled to fend for himself, but his incapacity for work quickly reduces him to an impoverished state. Physically and morally debilitated by the experiences of his early years, he is unprepared to struggle for his place in the sun. Vasco is his only friend, as he lacks the ability to communicate his feelings to anyone else. Poverty, isolation, disease—this is the triad of forces in which Ferruccio is hopelessly entangled. In January, 1945, he develops an intestinal ailment, which the doctors are unable to diagnose, and after a six-month battle for survival, Ferruccio dies.

Pratolini's interpretation of his brother's life must be seen first in relation to the theme of *Il Quartiere: Il Quartiere* is concerned in part with adolescence itself, that transitional and in many respects decisive time in the life of a human being during which the advent of sexual maturity usually coincides with a need to acquire independence of mind and spirit, to explore the world, and to rebel against parental authority and develop ideas and attitudes of one's own. But this process must unfold within a concrete social context, and in *Il Quartiere* Pratolini constantly stresses the sense of communal solidarity which animates the boys and girls of Santa Croce. Ferruccio's adolescence was devoid of warmth and friendship. His spirit languished in total submission to the will of the major-domo, his servant-master:

> The conditions of your childhood continued into your adolescence: you never discovered anything with your own eyes. Thus you lived always alone, but not alone with yourself, alone with him; your thoughts were those that he suggested. (p. 42)

All of the characters in *Il Quartiere* have one need in common, the need to be respected by their peers, to belong to some social or political group that trusts and esteems them. It is this need that Ferruccio was never able to satisfy:

> You could find nothing to lean on, you lacked the confidence that comes to a man—and you were already twenty—from a society that has seen him born and raised, in the midst of which he has spent his life, and by virtue of which he feels himself supported by communal solidarity —or even, perhaps, opposed by a disapproval that is itself an incentive to fight for his daily bread. . . . Your soul had undergone too violent a trauma, so that your days were now a series of painful human collisions from which, invariably, you emerged wounded. (pp. 111–12)

During his childhood and adolescence, Vasco's feelings toward his brother oscillate between pity and hatred. He pities his brother because he senses that Ferruccio is being smothered by the oversolicitous adults who are caring for him. But he also hates Ferruccio, a hatred rooted in his conviction that Ferruccio caused the death of his mother. For many years he continues to associate the fact of Ferruccio's existence with the death of his mother, and it is precisely this association which prevents him from loving his brother. Between 1924 and 1932, the two brothers see each other rarely as they live in two entirely different worlds. Vasco becomes convinced that he is not his brother's keeper. The allure of worldly success, his literary and political activities, his evenings spent drinking and gambling with friends finally make him forget Ferruccio atogether.

One day in 1935 (Ferruccio is now seventeen, Vasco twenty-two) the two brothers meet accidentally in a pool room, but Vasco does not acknowledge Ferruccio. For a variety of reasons—shame, embarrassment, a sense of acute discomfort at suddenly being confronted with the awareness of his failure as a brother—he pretends that he doesn't know Ferruccio. But this painful episode marks a turning point in the relationship between the brothers. Several weeks later Ferruccio comes to visit Vasco at his apartment on via Ricasoli, and immediately, as if only in that moment did they discover their common origin and destiny, the alienation between them is dissolved. They talk freely of their mother, about their ailing grandmother with whom they later spend their evenings together, and about their hopes and ambitions. Then Vasco contracts tuberculosis. At this point in the narrative Pratolini indicates that the physical fact of his blood relationship with Ferruccio turned into something much more significant, namely the spiritual sense of brotherhood, the bond of human solidarity linking two men now fully aware of their love for each other:

> I had to stay two years in the sanatorium, between mountains and a lake. We wrote to each other often. You had had to interrupt your studies and were working in an office. Your letters were like you: timid, shy, undemonstrative, yet teeming with affection and generosity. I recognized in them one of the things that attached me to life. One of the essentials. (p. 104)

A truthful and eloquently simple story of the unfolding of love between two brothers, Cronaca familiare also expresses the human values in Pratolini's other works of this period, particularly Cronache di poveri amanti.

Cronache di poveri amanti [21] was written between February and August, 1946, and published in the spring of 1947. It must be remembered that for Pratolini the word cronaca had special meanings and reverberations derived from his reading of the medieval Florentine chroniclers, particularly Dino Compagni. For Pratolini, Florence was an ill-starred city, its people condemned by the ineluctable law of its own nature to unceasing violence and conflict. This idea was forcefully expressed by Pratolini in an article which appeared in the magazine Il Politecnico in December, 1947:

> Guelfs and Ghibellines, Whites and Blacks, bourgeoisie and proletariat, tore each other apart for 400 years. . . . The Florentine people has been made expertly acute by sacrifices and betrayals that have occurred in all centuries. It doesn't believe in revealed truths. Its chronicles record a continuous succession of personal disputes, of quarrels and conflicts between individuals, quarters, and political parties that involve the Universe: the Divine Comedy is

the private invective of an exile against the dominant faction . . .

In effect, the political struggle between fascism and anti-fascism, during the years 1919 to 1925, assumed immediately the character of "factional warfare" (lotta di parte). Almost at once the square came on to the scene, along with ambush, assassinations, fierce ridicule, and the jeering contempt of the victors for the vanquished. . . . In Florence, fascism imposed itself in the same way that the Guelfs gained power, with the physical elimination of their adversaries, with terror.[22]

Cronache begins in May, 1925, and in the first three chapters, Pratolini introduces or briefly alludes to many of the more than fifty characters who play their various parts in his chronicle. The great majority of these characters are residents of via del Corno, a narrow, obscure, impoverished street located not far from Palazzo Vecchio. Among the most important are the coaldealer Egisto Nesi and his son Otello; four adolescent girls, "the guardian angels" of via del Corno, named Milena, Bianca, Clara, and Aurora; Mario Parigi, a printer's apprentice who hails from Santa Croce; the blacksmith Corrado, nicknamed Maciste, and his wife Margherita; Ugo Poggioli, an itinerant fruit vendor; Carlino Bencini, an insurance clerk and fanatical Fascist who has taken a young man named Osvaldo Liverani under his wing; and "La Signora," a clever and vindictive woman who plots to evict the *cornacchiai*, but who is ultimately reduced to a state of blubbering idiocy by a stroke. The Signora is for a time assisted in her conspiratorial machinations by Gesuina, an orphaned country girl whom the Signora adopted when she was a child, and who now acts as her spy.

The "Night of the Apocalypse," described in Chapter 14, is the central and climactic episode of the novel. It is early October, 1925, and Maciste, Mario, Bruno, and Otello are paying cards at Maciste's apartment. At about eight o'clock, Revuar and the cobbler Staderini arrive suddenly and tell them that a group of Fascists have set out on a punitive expedition against some "subversives." Maciste immediately concludes that the subversive the Fascists are after is his comrade Tribaudo. Ugo arrives and tells Maciste that he has just forcibly extracted information from Osvaldo to the effect that Tribaudo is only one of several subversives whom the Fascists intend to assassinate that night. The two men set out on Maciste's side-car to warn Tribaudo and the others. They accomplish their mission, but the squad car carrying the Fascists, among whom are Carlino and Osvaldo, catches up with them at Piazza San Lorenzo. One of the squadrists aims and fires, and Maciste is struck in the back of the neck and dies instantly. Ugo is wounded, but he manages to escape. He later becomes a trusted member of the Communist Party and, of equal importance, through his love for Gesuina liberates her from the Signora's tyranny.

In the concluding chapters of the novel, Pratolini describes the triumph of the Fascist regime and its impact on the lives of Ugo, Gesuina, Bruno, Milena, Mario, and the other residents of via del Corno. It is now the winter of 1926, and the Fascist era has begun in earnest. Carlino struts about and is feared by everyone. Osvaldo has become a trusted member of the party, despite his former revisionist tendencies. Order and authority are firmly established. Ugo is arrested and sentenced to five years in prison. Mario, too, is tried for subversion, but is released because of insufficient evidence, and he and Milena leave for France. But dictatorship and terror do not arrest the flow of life on via del Corno. In the final scene, Renzo, a newcomer to the street, meets Musetta, Aurora's younger sister. Pratolini's chronicle comes to a close as the two youngsters talk about their hopes, their plans for the future, about the events of via del Corno, and about "life."

In view of the fact that via del Corno is the main setting of *Cronache*, it is fitting that the novel should begin with a description of the street, and with references to some of its inhabitants. In pages characteristic of the descriptive technique he uses in this novel, Pratolini presents us with a series of precise references to the sights, sounds, and smells of via del Corno, on an evening in May, 1925. The novel begins as follows:

> The lamp outside the Cervia Hotel was at last extinguished and the cock on Nesi the coaldealer's roof had just crowed. The passing of the tramcar bringing the drivers home from night duty woke up Oreste the barber in his shop in the Via dei Leoni, where he slept, some fifty

yards away from Via del Corno. Today was market day, and his first client would be the *fattore*, the country overseer from Calenzano, who appeared at Oreste's shop every Friday morning with a week's growth on his cheeks. On the Torre di Arnolfo the pennant bearing the Florentine lion was flying toward the east and promised fine weather. In the little alleys behind the Palazzo Vecchio the cats had begun to scratch open the paper parcels of garbage. The houses were so close to each other across the narrow street that the moonlight only just managed to brush the windowpanes of the top stories, but Nesi's cock, perched on the high terrace, saw it and gave vent to his feelings.

Now that the hotel lamp in the Via del Corno was switched off, the only remaining light came from the window of the Signora, who passed the night nursing the sores in her throat. Maciste's horse pawed the ground restlessly from time to time, behind the forge where it had its stall. It was May. There was no trace of a breeze, and the still night air exhaled foul odors: a heap of manure from the horses that had been shod during the day lay in front of the blacksmith's door, and the dumps and parcels of domestic refuse had been spread outside the other doors as usual. The little privy at the corner of the street was completely hidden by rubbish and had been so for months. (pp. 3–4)

But in these same opening pages one notes immediately that Pratolini does not intend to limit his depiction of life on via del Corno to a series of picturesque if realistic "street scenes." After describing the street itself, he introduces a motif, recurrent throughout the novel, that symbolizes one of the many forces of established authority with which the poor people of via del Corno must contend: the police patrol headed by the ubiquitous and unnamed "Brigadiere." Two of the *cornacchiai*, Nanni and Giulio, are on parole. Hence the "Brigadiere" and several of his aides make a nightly visit to the street to check on the whereabouts of the parolees. But Nanni and Giulio are not the only ones on probation on via del Corno: "in the Via del Corno all who hearken to the sergeant's 'Good night' are subconsciously on probation." (p. 13)

Gradually, as Pratolini begins to recount the various *cronache*, and as he shifts back and forth from person to person, from scene to scene, and from incident to incident, more and more aspects of life on via del Corno are brought to the reader's attention. We learn, for example, that for the young lovers, Bruno and Clara, Mario and Bianca, Otello and Aurora, "Via del Corno was the most glamorous street in the world, because it was their street, where they lived and could gaze at each other from their windows." For Luisa Cecchi, notwithstanding the fact that she lives continuously on the very edge of penury, via del Corno is the world, the universe, where she finds her happiness. Luisa's sentiments are shared by the majority of the *cornacchiai,* and in particular by the four "guardian angels" of the street, Milena, Bianca, Clara, and Aurora. The four adolescent girls do not like Crezia Nesi, however, the wife of the coaldealer, because Crezia

> was a woman of the people, whose husband's fortune had turned her head, she never returned anyone's greeting when she went out, and always held her handkerchief to her nose until she had reached the Piazza della Signoria. (p. 57)

Friendliness is one of the very few prerequisites for acceptance by the people of via del Corno. They live together as a small community and therefore expect their neighbors to be truly neighborly.

It is precisely because the people of via del Corno live in such close physical proximity that the normal human fondness for gossip becomes, on this street, almost a way of life, at once a diversion and a necessity. News travels at lightning speed on via del Corno. But this gossipiness, a characteristic trait of the *cornacchiai,* is rarely malicious in intent. There is a true feeling of human solidarity in them that precludes a mere prying into other people's business for its own sake. One episode in particular illustrates how the ethic of interdependence and solidarity manifests itself in *Cronache* in concrete, dramatic terms. Milena, one of via del Corno's guardian angels, has recently moved away from the street and is living with her husband, Alfredo, in another section of the city. Alfredo, who owns a grocery store, would prefer to dissociate himself from politics. But, like every character in *Cronache,* he discovers that noninvolvement is impossible in the new

Fascist era. When asked by Carlino why he has not yet contributed his dues to the local Fascist party headquarters, Alfredo replies that he has the right to spend his money in whatever way pleases him and Carlino should mind his own business. Several days later he decides that he had better accede to Carlino's wishes, but before he arrives at party headquarters with the money he is savagely beaten by a group of blackshirts. Milena waits for him at their store until two o'clock in the morning. Then, unable to repress her fears any longer, she rushes to her mother's apartment. The people of via del Corno respond almost as one choral, unanimistic voice to Milena's cry for help:

> It was Maciste who first heard Milena's voice calling "Mama!" from the street below. It was two o'clock in the morning, the hour when sleep is deepest, but one's own child's cry is an angel's trump that would have awakened Christ himself from the dead. A second later Gemma was at the window, frozen with fear.
> "Mama, open!"
> "My soul, what's happened?"
> "Alfredo hasn't come home!"
> Their voices woke up the entire Via del Corno. On a summer night who would give a second thought before jumping out of bed on such an occasion? Clorinda proved the most agile, followed by the Staderinis, by Lando, and by Rosetta, who peered from her little porthole in the attic room of the Cervia to which Ristori had banished her. Within two minutes heads were bobbing at every window, and surprise and conjecture ran the whole length of the street. But Milena had disappeared up her mother's stairs, and details were sorely lacking. Bianca wanted to go over and knock, but her father stopped her.
> "Someone should do something," said Fidalma. "They are two lone women."
> The circumstances, however, were considered delicate, and only someone who was really intimate could possibly interfere—Margherita, in this instance. (pp. 102–3)

The people of via del Corno are for all practical purposes powerless to defend and assert their interests as a collective unit, for amost all of them belong to Florence's lumpen-proletariat. They do have several weapons of defense, however, among which is the refusal to extend their customarily friendly greetings to people who violate the elementary code of solidarity on which their life together is based. To betray the ethic of solidarity that governs life on via del Corno (the Fascist Carlino and the thief Nanni), or to exploit it for one's own selfish purposes (the Signora), is to lose the respect and friendship of the *cornacchiai*. When they learn that Carlino has been indirectly responsible for the attack on Alfredo, all of the *cornacchiai* except Nanni and the hotel proprietor Ristori refuse to acknowledge his presence as he struts down the street. Nanni, never greatly admired by the *cornacchiai* because of his exploitation of Elisa, one of the prostitutes of the Albergo Cervia, had nevertheless been accepted as a member of the community. But when it is learned that he has been acting as one of Carlino's informers, he is immediately cast into moral exile by via del Corno.

A multitude of small, sometimes trivial, facts make up the *cronaca* of life on via del Corno. But this *cronaca*, even the most inconsequential aspects of it, serves an important thematic function in the novel, namely to point up the idea of the life force itself in its most humble and commonplace forms. Pratolini sees via del Corno as a microcosm of an impoverished but resilient humanity. A sense of human solidarity, friendliness, warmth, wit— these are the virtues of the *cornacchiai* which Pratolini celebrates in *Cronache*.

Pratolini represents the conclusions regarding communism and fascism, justice and injustice, good and evil, which the poor people of via del Corno ultimately reach, as based entirely on their judgments of Maciste and Carlino. They judge human beings, not ideologies, acts, not doctrines. It is impossible, therefore, to speak of the political struggle in *Cronache* without at the same time speaking of the personal values and commitments of the people engaged in this struggle.

If a novel as unanimistic in spirit as *Cronache* can be said to have a "hero," it is the Communist blacksmith, Maciste. Maciste is a prototype of the Pratolinian hero in that virtually all of his actions, whether in personal relationships, work, or politics, are motivated essentially by love and friendship. Not all the men he saves from Fascist violence are Communists, but all are anti-Fascists, and this factor certainly contributes to Maciste's decision to help them. Fundamentally they are men in danger, and Maciste's primary commitment is to the sanctity of life. His politics is the politics of love.

In his portrayals of Ugo and Mario, both of whom follow Maciste's example and become trusted members of the anti-Fascist underground, Pratolini emphasizes the fact that their political commitments also stem from a primary belief in love. When Mario first comes to via del Corno in the fall of 1925, he is still a quite innocent young man. Though an orphan, he gives the appearance of a person who has never been touched by tragedy, and who looks on life as a simple matter of adjusting oneself to events as best one can. He forms an attachment for Bianca, and thinks seriously about marrying her. But Bianca turns out to be a childishly sentimental and somewhat superficial girl, and Mario concludes that he could not be happy with her. His realization that Bianca could never become the ideal mate for whom he is looking, marks the beginning of his development into manhood, a process that is accelerated by Maciste. Whenever the opportunity presents itself, Maciste questions Mario about his political attitudes. In a scene that is among the most memorable in *Cronache*, Pratolini pictures Maciste and Mario talking together as they ride to the outskirts of the city on Maciste's motorcycle:

> Maciste would slow the bike down to walking speed, push back the goggles from his eyes, and let fall a word or two.
> "Well, have you been to see Carlino at Fascist headquarters yet?" he asked the first time.
> "No, I haven't," replied Mario vehemently, "and I shan't go either, I don't like his face."
> "But he's one of the most hard-boiled Fascists."
> "I'm quite sure he is, but he's a ruffian. The ideal is something quite different."
> "Let's hear it, then."
> "It's the revolution which you Reds weren't capable of bringing about."
> "And who stopped us? Wasn't it the Fascists?"

"You were afraid of the Royal Guard and the *carabinieri*. You must admit that the Fascists beat you on your own revolutionary ground."

"But the Fascists were on the side of the Royal Guard and the *carabinieri*, weren't they?"

"You always answer by asking another question. Tell me truthfully, has fascism restored order or not?"

"That's what I'm asking you. Who upset the order? And then this fascism of yours—is it merely order, or is it also a revolution?"

"The revolution is still under way. Sooner or later the bosses will have to recognize it."

"But tell me, who's supposed to bring about the revolution?"

"The people—we workers."

"Right you are; then how many of all the workers in your printing shop are on the Fascist register?"

Mario at once became serious, as though struck by a sudden thought. His face reflected the annoyance of one who, after a long search, finds what he is looking for standing right before his eyes.

"Ten out of a hundred and eighty," he replied.

At this juncture Maciste pressed the dagger home. "And who owns the printing works?"

"The man who manages it, along with his three sons and his sister-in-law, and," he added, "you guessed right—all five of them are Fascists."

Maciste withdrew his dagger and patted Mario on the back like a father. "Well, there we are," he said. "Shall we go for a spin now?"

When the bike was well under way, with the wind full in his teeth, Mario cried, "We must continue this discussion."

"We most certainly will," replied Maciste. He looked down at the boy's upturned face and smiled secretly beneath his goggles.

This conversation leaves a permanent mark on Mario. But it is not only his "conscience" which has matured. His "heart" keeps pace with the development of his political conscience. A significant indication of this is the relationship he establishes with Milena, the young widow of Alfredo the grocer who died of wounds inflicted on him by the blackshirts. Several months after the death of her husband, Milena becomes aware of her more than friendly interest in Mario. She feels guilty about this, and struggles to suppress her emotions. Yet her young heart clamors for love, and Mario has proven himself to be the kind of sympathetic and sincere man whom she admires.

Just as love, not Marxist doctrine, is the motive force in the lives of the three Communists, Maciste, Mario, and Ugo, so in the same way ideological considerations have little influence in determining the political allegiances of the two Fascists, Carlino and Osvaldo. Fascism, for Carlino, is a passion, not a cause or an idea:

> Good and evil often become confused where passion is involved; Carlino had surrendered himself body and soul to his own particular brand of passion. (p. 74)

A lust for violence, a warped conception of patriotic duty, and a need to be feared and respected are the distinguishing characteristics of this young spokesman for the Fascist revolution. Carlino is a Fascist because fascism provides him with a political justification for his deep-rooted lust for violence and power.

But the Signora represents an equally grave threat to the security and happiness of via del Corno. Like the dictator "Lui" who rules the nation, to whom she is compared, the Signora has a compulsive need to place herself at the center of the universe. The Signora, with her spies, her unearned wealth, her cravings and keen intelligence, is the ruler of via del Corno. She is malicious, hypocritical, and extraordinarily clever. A sexual pervert, she rationalizes her lesbian lusts by claiming that her love creates, while that of a man destroys. She is ruled by her appetites, which are insatiable, and by a feeling of vengeful wrath towards the whole world. She is alternately enfeebled and full of animal spirits, states of being that depend on the responses of the young woman or women unlucky enough to fall into her clutches. She worships power, money, and things, but above all power. From a political and moral standpoint, she is completely opportunistic. She is on excellent terms with both the police and the Fascists. Many of Pratolini's descriptions of her seem grotesque, almost dehumanized. Those passages in which she is compared to "He who rules the government of the nation" are more firmly grounded in precise and realistic observation:

> The Signora was a sensitive creature who had placed herself at the center of the universe. She had regulated her life according to her whims and personal needs. Incapable of seeing right and wrong objectively when something or someone crossed her path, she had always considered herself generous and loyal and at the same time betrayed and injured. That was why revenge was second nature to her. (p. 309)

Carlino and the Signora are among the characters in *Cronache* who function as symbolic representatives of those aspects of human psychology which, in Pratolini's interpretation, permitted fascism to take root and to thrive in Italy. They are portrayed as individuals, yet there can be no doubt that they are meant also to symbolize widely prevalent types.

Virtually every incident in this novel reflects Pratolini's origins as a Florentine and a proletarian. His "modern chronicle" unfolds during the years 1925 to 1927. But its setting and mood, the "nature" of its characters, the political conflicts in which they are engaged, remind us of Pratolini's conviction that "Florentine history from 1919 to 1945 was written by Dino Compagni 600 years ago."

Via del Corno is only one obscure street in an entire city that has played a "time-honored role in history, the memory of which every stone and every bell preserved." (p. 213) The terrible "Night of the Apocalypse," when Maciste and other anti-Fascists lost their lives, is simply a re-enactment of events that have occurred in Florence through the ages:

> The revolver shots and songs of the *squadristi* echoed in every street where the terror passed. The ruling factions of antiquity seemed to be repeating their massacres under the full moon. (p. 212)

It is not only in violent factional strife that, for good and for evil, the Florentines of the twentieth century remain true to their traditions. The annual *festa delle rificolone* during which the poor people of Florence give vent to their love of wit, satire, and ribaldry, is simply "Machiavelli's comedies played in the open air." (p. 159) Some of the inhabitants of via del Corno have the ready wit for which the Florentine people has been known since the time of Boccaccio. In the language of the cobbler Staderini, for example, one often hears an echo of Pulci's Margutte, as well as the sly, mordant wit of Stenterello.

Cronache is a felicitous synthesis of motifs which Pratolini began to explore as far back as 1936, in the story "A Memorable Day," and which he continued to treat from diverse points of view, and with varying degrees of artistic success, in *Via de' Magazzini, Le amiche,* and *Il Quartiere.* The instinctive group solidarity of the youngsters portrayed in "A Memorable Day," the sense of interdependence that unites the members of an impoverished Florentine family in *Via de' Magazzini,* the melancholy tales of poor lovers recounted in *Le amiche,* and the feeling of communal loyalty which animates the adolescents of *Il Quartiere,* are all interwoven into this chronicle of Florentine proletarian life under Fascist domination. The novel has its limitations, of course. Pratolini succeeds for the most part in convincing us that each person and situation has a definite thematic function to perform, but the chronicle is probably overladen with facts and trivia that might better have been discarded. Some of the character studies are intriguing and precise, but too many are hastily and sketchily executed. Yet despite these shortcomings, *Cronache* is a memorable work of art, and marks one of the high points in Pratolini's gradual evolution toward the novel of social realism embedded in historical fact.

Un eroe del nostro tempo,[23] written during the winter of 1947, less than six months after the completion of *Cronache,* was published in February, 1949. The names of Giuseppe Borgese and Italo Svevo have been mentioned by some critics as probable influences on this novel. Pratolini admired the work of these two novelists, as evidenced by one of his articles in *La Ruota* in 1942, in which he referred to them, along with Verga, Pratesi,

Tozzi, Palazzeschi, and Bacchelli, as writers who had given Italy a series of "indisputably significant novels." [24] It is apparent, however, that the examples set by two other writers, the nineteenth century Russian novelist Mikhail Lermontov and Pratolini's contemporary Alberto Moravia, were more decisive in determining the themes and methodology of the work.

Pratolini made an interesting reference to Moravia in an article entitled "Society and the Novel" which appeared in *Sempre Avanti!* in December 1947:

> The artist who consoles his readers is an inferior artist. To console people today is tantamount to accepting the barbarism that is in each one of us. . . . If each of us were able to judge himself objectively through other men, to make his own the sufferings and joys of others, to insert himself disarmed into human society, a great part of this barbarism would be stamped out. Therefore, from their opposed positions, Moravia and Vittorini are novelists who count today.[25]

Moravia is an uncompromising critic as well as acute observer of manners and morals. His tough-minded, analytical brand of realism provided Pratolini with a model to emulate.

Pratolini borrowed the title of his novel from the Russian novelist Lermontov, whose work was also an attempt to symbolize in one character certain moral and psychological defects which he saw as prevalent in the society of his time. Pechorin, Lermontov's "hero," combines the duplicity of the adult who uses his own and others' emotional weaknesses as tactical weapons to achieve his ends, with the sweet, beguiling innocence of a child. This mixture of astuteness and innocence is also a cardinal element in the personality structure of Sandrino, Pratolini's symbolic "hero of our time."

Un eroe differs in some important respects from all of Pratolini's preceding works. The sense of place has no importance whatever in *Un eroe*. As opposed to *Il Quartiere* and *Cronache*, which are diffuse, kaleidoscopic descriptions of life, *Un eroe* is compact and concentrated in structure. It has two principal characters, Sandrino and his mistress, Virginia. Every incident in the novel, as well as every other character, functions in relation to them. *Un eroe* contains no lyrical evocations of love and nature. Pratolini's prose in this work is cool and terse, qualities which are admirably suited to a predominantly psychological novel.

The central character and themes of *Un eroe*, on the other hand, can be related to easily identifiable antecedents in Pratolini's preceding works. Sandrino bears a striking resemblance to the Fascist Carlino of *Cronache*. Like Carlino, he is fully content only when he is inflicting pain on another human being. An act of violence, and especially one committed in the name of the Fascist cause in which he believes, represents the fulfillment of his deepest instinctual needs. The main themes of *Un eroe* were also explored previously by Pratolini. The themes of love, political struggle, and education are present in *Un eroe*, but since it is Sandrino's story that occupies the foreground of the narrative, these themes function in relation to him, and are therefore not as directly germane to Pratolini's artistic purposes as they are in *Il Quartiere* and *Cronache*.

Un eroe is composed of two parts. Part I opens in the fall of 1945 and is devoted in large measure to a description of the morbid relationship between Sandrino Vergesi, a sixteen-year-old disciple of Mussolini, and Virginia Aloisi, a submissive, defenseless woman of thirty-three who finds in her love for Sandrino the meaning and purpose of her life. Sandrino lives with his widowed mother in a two-room flat adjoining that of Virginia. The young Communist couple Bruna and Faliero live on the same floor of the apartment house. Faliero, who is acting as Sandrino's guardian, deduces from certain comments Virginia inadvertently makes that her interest in Sandrino is not maternal, as she claims, but sexual. He reveals his suspicions to his wife, Bruna, who decides to take immediate action and attempts, without success, to persuade Virginia to break her liaison with Sandrino.

Part II takes place in the early months of 1946. Sandrino absconds to Milan with Virginia's life savings, which he intends to use to purchase weapons for a new Fascist insurrection. In Milan he has a meeting at a prearranged place with three men who take the money, promising that they will use it to procure the weapons. Sandrino never hears from them again, and when he realizes that he has been tricked, he returns home. Upon his return he discovers that Virginia has departed without leaving word as to where she has gone and when, if ever, she will come back to him. In the middle of part II, the theme of Sandrino's possible re-education and redemption is announced. Faliero's sage counsel appears to have helped him understand himself. Then he meets Elena, a sensitive, intelligent girl of his own age, and for a time it seems that her friendship has also had a beneficial effect on him. But Virginia suddenly reappears and tells him how empty life has been without his love and affection. She is ready to forgive him for everything, if only he will care for her and the child she has conceived. Sandrino leads Virginia to a garden where many of their earlier rendezvous had taken place. He pushes her against an iron gate at the entrance to the garden, takes her neck in his hands and shoves it down with all his strength on the point of one of the iron bars. He leaves her there, grotesquely impaled. Thus ends Pratolini's story of a hero of our time.

The first part of *Un eroe*, devoted to the relationship between Sandrino and Virginia, is a compactly written description of two forms of human debasement which, in Pratolini's view, permitted fascism to triumph in Italy. Sandrino and Virginia complement each other. Sandrino is a sadist, Virginia a masochist. Sandrino must dominate, Virginia must be dominated. They also share a deep sense of loyalty to fascism, conditioned in both by the fact that persons dear to them had died for the Fascist cause. Sandrino's father was killed in Abyssinia in 1936, and in a last letter to his son had pleaded with him to remain loyal to the cause of Fascist imperialism. Virginia's husband, a prosperous engineer, was killed by the partisans in 1944, so that in her mind fascism represents security, prosperity, and domestic happiness, while anti-fascism means insecurity and loneliness. She allows herself to be tyrannized by Sandrino, for she is a pathetic creature willing to endure any indignity in order to feel loved and wanted. Painfully aware of her own inner emptiness, Virginia yearns to be completed by someone "stronger and wiser" than she. When Sandrino promises to love and protect her, Virginia concludes that "Even if she had wished to do so, she would never be able to free herself from his control." (p. 57) Lack of will is a quintessential element of Virginia's personality.

In the first part of the novel, Pratolini's symbolic hero of our time appears as a vicious animal. Sandrino is cunning, resourceful, and hostile. He is incapable of tenderness. This fact emerges very clearly in his conception of sex. Sandrino conceives of sexual intercourse as an act of violence, not of love; as an assertion of his complete mastery over another human being. Indeed, sex *is* violence, aggression, domination for our hero. He makes his sexual attitudes unmistakably clear to Virginia:

> For me to have a woman is like killing her. To feel a thing that defends itself and that you can crush, and crush, and crush until it has no more breath in it. (p. 114)

Another facet of Sandrino's personality at first seems incompatible with cruelty and guile, but, in view of his still tender years, is entirely believable, and makes the story of his life all the more tragic. In many instances Sandrino is sincere and spontaneous despite himself. He wishes to be in complete control of himself at all times, yet there is a residue of impulsiveness in his nature that he cannot suppress. It is this facet of his personality, combined with his boyishly innocent appearance, which accounts for the strangely ambivalent feelings of Bruna and Elena toward him, and proves ultimately to be at once the potential source of his redemption and the cause of his and Virginia's destruction:

> He was constantly assailed by feelings which were objective, even if cruel, by aspirations which were sometimes puerile and inhuman, but always the result of reflection, which, however, he very frequently forgot almost deliberately in order to concern himself with the most immediate impulse, with the most undisciplined feeling. (p. 156)

This is the crux of Sandrino's dilemma. He is cruel and cunning, but also pathetically vulnerable.

But *Un eroe* is not only a psychological study of a neurotically disturbed adolescent boy. Sandrino is not an isolated, possibly pathological "case" of interest only to students of abnormal behavior, but rather symbolic of vices and warped attitudes which were, presumably, widely prevalent in the society of his time. Evidently Pratolini felt that the characteristics of the time, from October, 1945, to the winter of 1946, were too well known to require examination, for he does not deal with them at all. It is precisely because Pratolini took these characteristics for granted that Sandrino's presumed typicality is not effectively demonstrated. It is probable that the episode describing the deal Sandrino makes with the three men who betray his trust is designed to suggest something of the utterly corrupt, self-seeking machinations of men who use the political loyalties of naïve adolescents to gain profit for themselves. If with this episode Pratolini intended to convey the degeneration of moral standards in certain segments of Italian society immediately after the war, then he should have expanded it by telling us more about the precise political and social conditions which made this type of exploitation possible. As it is, we are left with the feeling that this chicanery is merely an isolated example of fraud, and bears no relation to a more general, factually grounded commentary on postwar life in Italy.

The three characters upon whom devolve the responsibility of re-educating Sandrino represent little more than schematically conceived projections of praiseworthy ideas and attitudes which seem superimposed on the narrative. In order to make the theme of re-education and possible redemption plausible, Pratolini should have endowed these characters with an intellectual and moral stature that they simply do not possess. Bruna and Faliero are both singularly colorless figures, and the fact that love must be at the core of meaningful political ideology does not lead to a clarification of the problems inherent in Sandrino's tragedy. Faliero's judgments are absurdly simplistic. This is his diagnosis of Sandrino's problems:

> Society has made him what he is. He was only a restless boy, full of instincts, full of life. They made him believe that evil was good, and vice-versa, and he didn't have the possibility to reflect, because he was so anxious to move, to do something. The first steps he took were sufficient to

persuade him that he could already walk and run. Now he's walking, he's running and if someone intervenes he thinks the intervention is motivated by a desire to frustrate and deceive him. (p. 142)

"Society ... good and evil ... a boy ... full of instincts, full of life:" vast abstractions which leave no impression whatever on the reader's moral imagination. Nor does Falieri's characterization of Sandrino seem consonant with the image already created of him as a corrupted and corrupting victim of fascism, war, and social disorder.

Yet despite these grave shortcomings, *Un eroe* has an important place in Pratolini's artistic development. The two basic problems he poses for himself in this novel—to describe the psychic as well as social determinants of human behavior, and to create "typical" characters who embody widely prevalent attitudes—will continue to occupy his attention in *Le ragazze*, and will determine in large measure the angle of vision from which he describes various phases and aspects of Florentine life in the trilogy *Una Storia Italiana*.

Pratolini wrote *Le ragazze di San Frediano* in the early months of 1948, "in order to detoxicate myself ... after having lived for months in the presence of the shadow and the angry desolation of Sandrino." [26] The novel first appeared in the magazine *Botteghe Oscure* in the fall of 1949, and was published in book form by Vallecchi in 1952. [27]

La ragazze is set in the working class quarter of San Frediano during the latter months of 1946. It is the story of Aldo, nicknamed Bob, a "small-town Casanova," and his five lustry girl friends, Tosca, Gina, Silvana, Mafalda, and Bice. Each of the girls thinks that she is the one Bob intends to marry. The truth is that Bob intends to marry none of them, but derives immense pleasure from keeping them guessing as to which one he will utimately choose for his bride.

After establishing the essential facts of Bob's life—his extraordinary good looks, his average competence as an office worker, his last-minute participation in the Resistance, his indifference to politics and total lack of working-class consciousness—Pratolini proceeds to describe the technique Bob uses in his many amatory exploits. The girls' responses to his maneuvers and infidelities constitute the other basic motif of the story. First we see Bob capturing the heart of one of his victims, then we see the victim react with disappointment, anger, and resentment when Bob abandons her in his incessant search for new conquests. The whole question is: will the girls realize they have been exploited, resolve their conflicts of interest, and express their wrath united and strong? Pratolini leaves no doubt in our mind that they will succeed in doing this, and with a vengeance. The five girls do in fact mete out stern justice to poor Bob. He goes to the park one night to keep a rendezvous with one of his sweethearts, but finds all five waiting for him. They insist that he choose, once and for all, the girl whom he intends to marry. When Bob refuses to change his habitually supercilious manner, they pounce on him, throw him to the ground, remove his pants, and expose his private parts with frenetic glee. Bob, shamed and humiliated, finally does marry one of the girls, Mafalda. One feels certain that he will never again offend the dignity of the girls of San Frediano, for the lesson they have taught him in the park has made him a sadder, but infinitely wiser man.

The key passage in Pratolini's character study of Bob appears in chapter six:

> considered objectively, he was only a young man a bit vain, adventurous within measure, who calculated the limits of his own imprudence, a little Casanova of the suburbs who lacked—besides genius and foolhardiness—the original virtue of the great lover: the need and the desire for full possession. (p. 28)

Bob is not highly sexed. The physical possession of his female admirers is therefore not his goal. His tactics are of cerebral, not visceral, origin. He is the male counterpart of the infamous "teaser" with whom every hot-blooded young man is only too familiar. Aside from his good looks, Bob is an irremediably average, mediocre fellow. He joined the partisans only after the dangerous street fighting had ended, and for primarily opportunistic motives. Realizing that his reputation as a virile Casanova would be endangered if he remained uncommitted to

either side, he chose to identify himself with the Resistance fighters only because the majority of Sanfredianini
were anti-Fascist. He is a bland mediocrity in his work,
and colorlessly neutral in his political attitudes. Everything he does is calculated to safeguard his reputation,
for he is devoid of intense feeling and incapable of performing any action that does not offer him immediate,
self-aggrandizing compensations.

Just as Bob's personality is the quintessence of proletarian mediocrity, so Mafalda, in her courage and pride,
typifies the best qualities of the working girls of San
Frediano. According to Pratolini's interpretation, these
qualities derive above all from their awareness that they
are citizens of a working-class quarter with a long tradition of militant independence; a tradition which they
revere and intend to continue. Tosca reminds Bob to
treat her with respect:

"I'm a San Frediano girl, and don't you forget it." (p. 9)

When Gina discovers that she has been rejected by Bob,
she instinctively reverts to type, and exclaims:

"I was a real San Frediano girl, as proud as the rest of
them, and now I've become your dummy, your helper, and
you couldn't have made me anything worse." (p. 75)

Mafalda challenges the other girls to teach Bob a lesson
he'll never forget by saying:

"we wouldn't be worthy of San Frediano if we didn't
skin him alive." (p. 90)

And, finally, when all conflicts of interest have been resolved, the girls march off together, determined at long
last to take justice in their own strong hands:

The girls of San Frediano marched to the offensive,
tough and lovely as their mothers had been. . . . They were
a circle around him, their hands in the air, their faces
burning. (p. 107)

Pratolini pays little attention to the individual personalities of the girls. One of the weaknesses of the book is
precisely this lack of sharp character differentiation. The
girls have the same beliefs and express themselves in the

same pungent manner. Nevertheless, as a collective portrait of a group of fiercely proud women, *Le ragazze* has
an undeniable originality and authenticity.

The story of Bob and the girls is set against the background of proletarian life in San Frediano. In the first
introductory chapter Pratolini describes its precise physical location, the various trades and occupations of its
people, its antiquity and squalor, and a host of other facts
which establish the identity of the quarter. The most
significant characteristic of the people of San Frediano
is that

> their participation in historic events has been intelligent
> and constant, even prophetic at times, though perhaps
> disordered. (p. 2)

This is precisely what distinguishes San Frediano from
Santa Croce and via del Corno. The people of San
Frediano have never been, like the Santa Croceans and
the *cornacchiai*, "betrayed by their own ignorance," but
rather have been stalwart and organized defenders of
their rights and interests. Since the days of Boccaccio,
and perhaps even before Boccaccio's time, the Sanfredianini have stood at the vanguard of the Florentine working class's struggles:

> Precisely because the foundation of their spirit is paved
> with incredulity, they are obstinate and active; and their
> participation in historic events has been intelligent, con-
> stant, even prophetic at times, though perhaps disordered.
> They have only covered over with more modern ideals their
> myths and banners; their lightheartedness, their intransi-
> gence, and their prejudices have remained the same.
> (pp. 2-3)

The phrase "participation in historic events" is of crucial importance, for in all of Pratolini's preceding works,
his characters strive fundamentally to adapt themselves
to historical change, and play no significant role in the
political and social events of their lives. They are involved in, and react to, events, at times heroically, as in
the case of Giorgio and Maciste, but do not initiate or
create them. *Le ragazze* foreshadows a basic shift of emphasis and perspective on Pratolini's part; in *Metello*
(volume I of *Una Storia Italiana*), which is also set

mainly in San Frediano, he will, for the first time in his career, concern himself with the struggles of the *organized* working class.

IN 1956 Pratolini collaborated with the painter Paolo Ricci in publishing an anthology of the works of the Neapolitan poet Raffaele Viviani. In his critical introduction, Pratolini contrasts Viviani's art with that of two other Neapolitan poets, Ferdinando Russo and Salvatore Di Giacomo, in much the same way as he had contrasted Mario Pratesi with other Tuscan provincial novelists. He makes a sharp distinction between the "authentic poetry" of Viviani and the mere picturesque word paintings of Russo and Di Giacomo. It is difficult to say with certainty whether or not Pratolini was thinking of himself while writing his introduction to Viviani's works, but certainly the following observations are as true of Pratolini, at least during the period we have just discussed, as they are of the Neapolitan poet:

> For both Russo and Di Giacomo, Naples and its people were a pretext for poetry; the object, let us say, not the subject of their inspiration.
>
> Viviani, on the other hand, does not stand at the window like Di Giacomo, nor does he come down to the street like Russo; he was born and grew up in the slums of Naples. This is his limitation, but it is also his strength. His poetry is not merely the consequence of an attentive and illuminating observation, nor is it the result of a lyrical transfiguration of Neapolitan reality. From the very beginning reality presented itself to his consciousness as a natural phenomenon: he was in the midst of it, he lived it. It never occurred to him that he could escape from this reality, or that he would say anything that was not inspired directly by the life, the events, the people of a Naples of which he himself was a character . . .[28]

If we substitute Pratolini for Viviani, and change the word Naples to Florence, we have a singularly accurate characterization of Pratolini's art during the years 1943 to 1950. In conclusion we can do no better than repeat a phrase used by the critic Luigi Russo with respect to the author of *Cronache di poveri amanti*: "Vasco Pratolini, the poet of his quarter." [29]

5 AN ITALIAN TALE
(1950–1960)

IN 1950, Pratolini began working on a cycle of novels, entitled *Una Storia Italiana*, a project which absorbed most of his creative energies during the decade from 1950 to 1960. Influenced by nineteenth and twentieth century realists and naturalists, in particular Balzac, Zola, Dreiser, Martin du Gard, and Sholokhov, Pratolini set himself the task of describing various aspects and phases of Italian life from 1875 to 1945. *Una Storia Italiana* is a trilogy, the first two volumes of which, *Metello* [1] and *Lo scialo*,[2] were published respectively in 1955 and 1960. The third volume, which has been tentatively entitled *I fidanzati del Mugnone*, is scheduled to appear in 1965.

Beginning in 1950, and thereafter almost annually, Pratolini made a series of lengthy journeys outside of Italy, the most important of which was to East Germany and Poland in 1956. Nine months after his return from Poland, Pratolini published an article entitled "Questioni sul realismo" in *Tempo Presente* in which he admitted that he had been aware of the "errors" of Stalinism long before the events in Poznan and Budapest, but that he had not had the moral courage to take a firm stand against these errors until the outbreak of violence shook the Communist world in the fall of 1956. In this same article Pratolini made an important declaration of intellectual independence from the "political and cultural line of the Italian Communist party":

> In effect, the events about which we are speaking have been profoundly, even if tragically, beneficial: after the first moment of anguish, rather than generate disorienta-

tion, they favored clarification, reawakened energies, stirred up already fruitful debates and arguments. . . . In order to establish the points of clarification, I will cite, in the first place, that no writer of any weight, young or not so young, committed to the Marxist ideology or at any rate to a particular leftist attitude, has avoided the responsibility of taking a position. This is not necessarily attesting to anti-Communist positions. Only the McCarthys of our own house can hope for the isolation of the Communist party as a political and ideological force. It is rather an affirmation of one's independence from the political and cultural line of the Italian Communist party. That later the PCI put its own militants on guard against this attitude, which it defined as "paternalistic," or in the best of cases "sentimental," is another proof, together with Togliatti's writing in *Irodalmi Ujsag*, not of its incapacity but of its refusal to understand both the figure and the true function of the artist in Socialist society itself. . . .

Thus we must never tire of condemning and protesting, in the name of Tibor Dery and of his comrades today imprisoned in Hungary, in the name of Harich and his comrades today imprisoned in East Germany. This doesn't mean passing over to the side of Franco, to the side of the Unamerican Activities Committee, to the side of the Holy Office and of its Italian organs of censorship; it means supporting socialism by denouncing errors and crimes when they happen; not afterwards, now.[3]

The ideas and feelings expressed by Pratolini in *Tempo Presente* illustrate the most striking characteristic of Italian cultural life during the 1950's, namely the psychology of crisis, the sense that the convictions and certainties of the war years, when one was either Fascist or anti-Fascist, were no longer applicable. This widespread sense of crisis gave rise in the 1950's to an attitude of detachment and disengagement. A more reflective, analytical mood replaced the enthusiasms of the immediate postwar years. Literary problems and movements were subjected to the same scrutiny as were political ideologies and social institutions. Indeed, after 1950 many Italian writers and critics began to express increasingly negative opinions of the neo-realistic movement. As we shall see,

Pratolini, too, was aware of neo-realism's shortcomings. In fact, what he calls his "change of direction" in 1950 from "chronicle" to "history" [4] coincided with, and to a certain extent was caused by, the "crisis" of neo-realism, which was referred to by a few of Carlo Bo's correspondents in *Inchiesta sul neorealismo* (1951).

The crisis of neo-realism was an important factor in determining Pratolini's decision to undertake a novelistic reconstruction of Italian life from 1875 to 1945. Unlike some of his colleagues, most notably Elio Vittorini and Carlo Bernari, Pratolini did not make an all-out attack on neo-realism. On the contrary, he was quick to defend its positive accomplishments. But he did recognize that after the liberation, Italian novelists had run the risk of replacing the preciosities of art prose with the possibly more deleterious rhetoric of protest and engagement. The gravest shortcoming of neo-realist novels and films was, in Pratolini's opinion, their lack of historical perspective; and it was precisely his awareness of this shortcoming which helped him reach a clear understanding of what his artistic methods and aims would be in *Una Storia Italiana*. The effects of war and social disorder had been vividly documented by the neo-realists, yet Pratolini saw that they had not concerned themselves directly with the causal nexus linking Italy's present to its past. In an interview with the critic Carlo Bo in July, 1960, Pratolini made explicit reference to the fact that the crisis of neo-realism coincided with the genesis of *Una Storia Italiana:*

> The crisis of neo-realism, which dates back to those years, like the suicide of Pavese and the industrious silence of Vittorini, coincide with my change of direction. Our works of that time endure because of the lyrical impetus and moral commitment with which they are infused. . . . Their limitation is their strength which permits them to endure because they are immersed without reservation in the waters (and in the blood) of a very specific period of our history; because they are the mirror, the voice of our conscience, partisan testimony, a bitter and burning act of exaltation and revelation of the hope and the horror of that particular Italy of that particular postwar era. And precisely of the disasters of war, of our long sickness and of our recovery

of health, portrayed at any rate in its visible, tangible effects. . . . But when the investigation of the effects was
finished, and when we were overwhelmed by a reality that
magnified these effects day by day, our work as writers ran
the risk of becoming identified with our daily obligation
to oppose and to protest. Now, for my part, I concluded
that to go back to the causes, to explain both their character and their significance, represented the most immediate, active, and useful thing that could be done.[5]

Pratolini's analysis of the shortcomings of neo-realism—
its lack of historical perspective and its subjective, "impressionistic" character—raises an important question:
What, in his opinion, are the fundamental constituents
of genuine literary realism? This question must be answered in as precise a manner as the few available documents will allow, since at the end of his interview with
Bo, Pratolini declared that

I was expecting you to ask me whether I thought that
with *Metello* and *Lo scialo* I had gone beyond neo-impres-
sionism and whether I had achieved a dimension of realism.
I would have answered that I think I approached it.

The particular "dimension" of realism that interests
Pratolini, and that he sought to achieve in *Una Storia
Italiana,* is social realism embedded in historically veri-
fiable fact. The principal characteristic of realism is that
it interprets society in dialectical terms, as a composite of
conflicts and contradictions in which the forces of good
and evil, progress and reaction, change and stasis are constantly interacting on each other. The purpose of realism
is therefore "to investigate reality in its contradictions, in
its good and evil, thereby giving us an image, partial but
not counterfeit . . . of the life and society of our time."
("Questioni sul realismo," p. 524.) Pratolini's conception
of the methodology of realism is directly dependent on
his view of its salient characteristic and purpose. Realism
presupposes in the first place an objective study of the
dominant social, political, and cultural events that characterize the historical period with which the novelist is
concerned. And since the realist aims to achieve an accurate representation of an historical epoch, he draws

many of his characters and episodes, and much of his background material, from real life. In his interview with Bo, Pratolini referred to this aspect of realism in commenting on his treatment of the first years of the Fascist epoch in *Lo scialo*. Many of the characters of that novel are drawn directly from life, and in some cases are either called by their real names or by names so close to the original that anybody familiar with the period in question would immediately recognize the character's identity. Certain of the characters and episodes in *Metello*, too, are taken directly from the pages of contemporary newspapers and from historical texts dealing with the era.

But notwithstanding the copious data gathered and included in *Una Storia Italiana*, neither of the two volumes thus far published is a merely photographic reproduction of reality. On the contrary, Pratolini ascribes great importance to the creative and symbolic components of literary realism. That Pratolini does not conceive of realism only in terms of its historical exactitude emerges very clearly in the article "Questioni sul realismo." The method and purpose of realism, as Pratolini interprets it, are:

> to uncover and reveal historical truth from the confused crisscrossing of daily events in which political man finds his motives; to express this truth through characters, which is to say to reinvent life; to draw from the imagination in such a way as to render this reinvention even less improbable and precarious than life itself; to use a language that, for being the language spoken by everyone, will have to become, in the final analysis, an exemplary language that nobody will ever speak. This is the achievement of Boccaccio, of Sacchetti, of Manzoni, of Verga. Realism consists of this, and as such excludes all mere nomenclature, . . . all hagiography, and all abstraction. It is, seemingly, the triumph of the conventional, but it is the triumph of the conventional, after you have persuaded yourself of the extreme freedom that the conventional affords, and with which it is nourished. Then it will appear to you as the triumph of imagination. (p. 525)

Realism, then, in Pratolini's view, is "the triumph of the conventional," and excludes, by its very nature, "all hagiography and all abstraction." In saying that realism excludes all hagiography Pratolini means that the realistic delineation of character can only be achieved by novelists who are conscious of the conflicting and often mutually contradictory ideas, impulses, and aspirations that influence the behavior of all human beings. Realism takes the full measure of a man, and therefore portrays his weaknesses as well as his strengths, his failures as well as his victories. The "hagiographical" idealization of character, whether in the name of a religion or of a political philosophy, is contrary to the essential nature of realism. As we shall see, this concept is particularly relevant to Pratolini's portrayal of Metello, the Socialist "hero of the collective," whose egotism and vanity often seem to overshadow his positive qualities.

The word "conventional" is for all practical purposes synonymous in Pratolini's mind with representative or typical. It is through a thorough and imaginative investigation of characters who typify widely prevalent attitudes that the realist creates a truthful image of the society of an historical epoch. The realist's point of departure is the individual, not the type. He proceeds from the particular to the general. He is interested in concrete human problems and situations. Hence realism "excludes all abstraction." But the novelist does not achieve an authentic "dimension" of realism unless he succeeds in creating characters who embody the typical characteristics of the society, and especially the class, to which they belong. A novel is realistic and historically valid to the extent that its characters are representative, not exceptional, products of their time.

The concept of typicality formed the basis of some explanatory comments Pratolini made in January, 1956 regarding the structure and conception of *Metello*, and in general of *Una Storia Italiana*. Speaking to a congress of construction workers, Pratolini referred to a letter he had received from a young Sardinian worker:

> He maintained that in the course of the novel one wasn't made sufficiently aware of the struggles that other categories of workers had to wage and that necessarily paralleled ... the political and organizational battles waged by the construction workers of that time.
>
> It was a seemingly unreasonable observation. I had

wanted to tell the story of a bricklayer, not of a ceramist, let us say, or of a mechanic, or of a smelter. Of course my intention was, through describing the experiences of Metello and his comrades, to reveal the typical life condition, the typical feelings, degree of emancipation, and level of class consciousness that animated the Italian proletariat at the beginning of this century. Therefore the story of the bricklayer Metello included ideally the story of a Metello smelter, a Metello ceramist, a Metello mechanic, and so on.

In truth, my intention was not so broadly ambitious; on the other hand, rather than ambition it is a question of a fundamental rule of the art of the novel: if a writer intends to base his work on the investigation and interpretation of reality, and does not want to detach himself, but on the contrary wants to confront directly the social conflicts that reality presents to his consciousness, he must be able to synthesize in the characters of his novel all of the characteristic and typical elements of the society that produces them.

You see, therefore, that in the light of these considerations, the criticism of the young Sardinian worker, instead of being unreasonable, becomes extremely acute; so acute, in fact, that if he were right, his criticism would raise serious questions concerning not the basic conception and structure of the novel, but its artistic result.[6]

The last sentence of the passage quoted above indicates that while Pratolini is perfectly willing to concede the possibility that in *Metello* he may have fallen short of realizing his artistic intentions, he has complete confidence in the correctness of the novel's "basic conception and structure." He has made similar comments concerning *Lo scialo*.

In the course of his interview with Carlo Bo, and in another conversation with Mino Guerrini, Pratolini explained the general structural and conceptual framework of *Una Storia Italiana* and indicated in precise terms why he chose particular character types and social classes as protagonists for each of the three volumes:

It was a simple, yet at the same time a difficult and exciting series of ideas that I had to articulate. The syphilis working in our blood between the two wars, and which from 1919 to 1945 we called fascism, . . . had not burst forth either in us or in our fathers; beneath this covering of social injustice, suppression of freedoms, and blunting of the human spirit, there was something we must have inherited. I concluded at that time (and it was not a great intuition, but rather a corollary of the premises) that our ills could be traced back to the years immediately following unification, which signified something on the map, but not in substance equality of rights and duties.

And I became convinced that this was the task I should set for myself: to move from intimate memories to chronicle to history, if you will; to document a reality investigated in and drawn from its strictly human origins more than from texts and oral tradition; to discover through the character investigated in his secret life, in his choral sorties, the most profound secret, perhaps the essential truth, of our national history.

During the Humbertine age, it was not the dominant moneyed classes, and the "historical contribution of the historic right," that brought Italy forward, that brought Italy into contact with the rest of Europe, but the working class, at its revolutionary dawn, with its first parties and organizations. . . . And not so much the working class in its "Socialist apostles" and in the souls of its libertarians . . . as in its totality of worker-citizens: their shock impact, their mortgage on the future. Even if in the last decades of the nineteenth century the working class did not hold power, it was nevertheless this class which set the dominant tone of the epoch with its leagues and labor unions. The theme of *Metello* was, more or less, that Crispi was not the representative man of that moment, but rather the young Turati.

Nor, from this point of view, had the preeminent role been played from 1910 to 1930 by the powerful bourgeoisie with its war shouted in the name of irridentism, with its fascism erected in the name of legality and order . . . , nor was it the working class, whose evolution and struggles, whose authentic and obscure heroism, had culminated in a terrible defeat, but it was rather the middle and petite bourgeoisie, with its delays and conformism, its quietism, its cult of domestic tranquility, its inextinguishable devotion to the strong, its rejection of its own popular origins and its aspiration to improve not so much its condition as its social status, that had formed the basis, the cowardly but stubborn, obtuse, timorous, calumnious army behind whose domestic bayonets fascism had established itself.

Finally, the secret and truest story of fascism, from Ethiopia to Spain to Dongo, is the story of the generation which grew up between the two wars, under fascism. It is the story of a generation which grew up under fascism, and which was therefore educated in a Fascist manner, and of its representatives who wanted to discover a truth, who had to struggle to emerge from darkness into light. All of this rendered, as in *Metello* and *Lo scialo*, through the private experiences of the characters ...

This was the way in which the idea of the trilogy took form in my mind.[7]

Besides being a lucid summary of the major premises and themes of *Una Storia Italiana*, the passages quoted above also clarify the ideological point of view from which Pratolini writes in each of the three volumes. *Metello* describes the "authentic and obscure heroism" of the Italian working-class movement "at its revolutionary dawn." *Lo scialo* is primarily the story of the petite bourgeoisie from 1910 to 1930, since it was this segment of the middle class which, in Pratolini's view, then moved to the forefront of Italian national life and with "its delays, its conformism, its cowardice and inextinguishable devotion to the strong," paved the way for the triumph of fascism. *I fidanzati del Mugnone* is the story of the Fascist generation itself, and is not so much concerned with the characteristics of a specific social class as with the moral and spiritual problems of a group of Florentine intellectuals who struggled "to emerge from darkness into light."

In regard to the question of literary sources for *Una Storia Italiana*, Pratolini sent me the following brief but illuminating statement in March, 1961.

> For the "sources" of *Una Storia Italiana*, why didn't you think of two writers about whom I must have spoken to you and who are not, in fact, any of those whom you mention. I mean Dreiser on the one hand and Roger Martin du Gard on the other. They are, obviously, "cultural" sources, elective affinities if you will. (And you might add, insofar as the "design" of *Una Storia Italiana*

is concerned, and above all in regard to *Metello*, Sholokhov.) Besides my eternal Balzac, naturally.

In the light of what has been said concerning Pratolini's
methodology in *Una Storia Italiana*, the emphasis he
places on tracing the private lives of individuals in relation
to various social classes and trends, and particularly his
interest in creating a broad, realistic picture of an historical epoch, it is not surprising that Balzac, Dreiser, Martin
du Gard, and Sholokhov, are among the writers with
whom he felt a strong "elective affinity."

Doubtless Balzac's broadly "sociological" vision of reality, his conception of life as a never-ending human comedy in which individuals played out their roles in accordance with their dominant passions and interests, exerted
a powerful influence on Pratolini's highly creative, but
always socially oriented, imagination. It is natural, also,
that Pratolini should have been attracted to Dreiser, for
like Dreiser he is a keen social observer and psychologist,
a Socialist with a warm faith in the working class, and
above all a novelist who aspires to create a "truthful image
of the life and society of our time."

Evidence of Pratolini's intense admiration for Roger
Martin du Gard appears in his article in *Tempo Presente*,
part of which he devoted to a general discussion of the
relationship between socialism and realism. After asserting
his belief that a writer could be a Socialist without being
a realist, and conversely a realist without being a Socialist,
Pratolini said that the two terms "socialism" and "realism" were most often incorrectly juxtaposed and mis-
takenly applied to western novelists for whom socialism
was a hope, not a reality. Still, he added, the western
world *had* produced a few novelists who could be legiti-
mately called both Socialists and realists. "Let us not
develop guilt and inferiority complexes that do not belong to us;" Pratolini said. "We have in the west enough
colossi to hold up mountains. One for everybody, Martin
du Gard." [8] Martin du Gard worked within the naturalist
tradition. He wrote a novel cycle depicting many facets
of French society during the period just preceding the
first World War. Yet perhaps of even greater interest
to Pratolini was the fact that Martin du Gard, despite

his preoccupation with political conflicts, diplomatic maneuvers, and revolutionary movements, never neglected
to focus his attention on the private lives of his characters;
their hopes and disappointments, their love affairs and
loneliness, their personal triumphs and tragedies. It is
this aspect of Martin du Gard's art which probably im-
pressed Pratolini most deeply.

It seems apparent that Pratolini used Sholokhov's *And
Quiet Flows the Don* as a model for the "design" of
Metello because *And Quiet Flows the Don*, like *Metello*,
depicts a society in transition. *Metello* deals with the rise
of the organized working-class movement in Italy just
after the struggle for unification, and treats of the conflict
in the minds of Metello and his fellow workers between
their attraction to anarchism (the past) and socialism
(the wave of the future). *And Quiet Flows the Don*
describes the impact of the Bolshevik revolution on the
people of the Don Cossack region of Russia, and derives
much of its power (thematically) from Sholokhov's skill-
ful treatment of his central characters' ambivalent attitude
toward Communist ideals because of their attachment
to the old, familiar ways of the past. In this sense the
parallel between the two works is clear. One might add
that Sholokhov's characters are never all black or all
white. His realism, like that of Pratolini, "excludes all
forms of hagiography."

Pratolini began writing *Metello* [9] in the summer of
1951 and completed his first draft in the fall of 1952.
During the next two years he made extensive revisions,
which were interrupted by other activities and commitments, so the novel was not published until February,
1955.

Metello is divided into four parts. Part I traces Metello's life from 1872, the year of his birth, to 1898. Metello,
an orphan, is taken into custody by a peasant family
named Tinaj, who live in Rincine, some thirty kilometers
from Florence. In 1885 the Tinaj family emigrates to
Belgium. Metello remains in Rincine, but instead of
going to work on one of the local farms, as had been
planned, he is seized by an impulse to return to the city
of his birth. A personable, resourceful lad, Metello is
befriended in Florence by an eccentric old anarchist

named Betto, who teaches him to read and write, and who familiarizes him with the rudimentary facts of life as lived by the Florentine working class. From that point on, Metello's life is determined by his contacts with various spokesmen for the new Socialist ideal, who convince him that the only hope for the workers lies in collective struggle. In 1898, Metello has two experiences that mark a decisive turning point in his career. The first is his meeting with Ersilia Pallesi, a proud daughter of San Frediano who later becomes his wife and loyal companion. The second is his participation in May, 1898, in a series of workers' demonstrations, as a result of which he is imprisoned for almost two years on the charge of sedition.

Part II opens in the year 1902, and Metello and Ersilia have been married for two years. Their baby boy, appropriately named Libero, is the first fruit of a union which proves to be founded on almost perfect physical and spiritual compatibility. Ersilia's strength of character, her resourcefulness, and above all her frankness and honesty, make her the ideal mate for Metello. Metello, now an experienced bricklayer and convinced Socialist, is at the age of thirty in the full flower of manhood. Yet certain of his weaknesses, particuarly his vanity and "Donjuanism," are still very much in evidence. In fact, these are precisely the weaknesses which will threaten the stability of his relationship with Ersilia.

Part III deals for the most part with the effects of a "legendary" forty-six day strike on the workers in general, and on Metello in particular. Metello, as one of the most articulate and respected members of the Labor League, is frequently called on to voice his opinions, and he resolutely takes his position as an *oltranzista*, that is, as one who wishes to see the strike through to the bitter end. But Metello, like many of his comrades, becomes restless. Unaccustomed to having so much time on his hands, he begins a flirtation with Ida Lombardi, the wife of a next-door neighbor. The flirtation quickly turns into an adulterous affair. Ersilia finds out about it, and gives Ida a severe thrashing. Metello later confesses his liaison and, without trying to justify his philandering, assures Ersilia that his "heart" had not been involved in the affair.

Part IV describes the last week of the strike, which culminates in outbreaks of violence between the *oltranzisti* and the *crumiri* (scabs), and between the workers and the soldiers, several of whom lose their tempers and fire at point blank range at their unarmed adversaries. Miraculously none of the workers is killed. At long last the bosses accede to the workers' demands. A new contract is signed, granting higher wages and somewhat better working conditions. But after victory is achieved, Metello and several of the other strike leaders are imprisoned for six months on the charge of "attempted rebellion against public order." They are ultimately absolved of the charge, however, and Metello and Ersilia resume their life together.

In considering the theme of Metello's education, it is important to know that Pratolini has a thesis to demonstrate in this novel, a thesis concerning the causes and significance of social progress. In chapter twelve, in referring to the workers' decision to strike for higher wages, Pratolini states:

> What was it then if not history, or progress, that was marching? They could be temporarily halted, but it was no longer possible to push them back. The machines that had been placed in their hands, and that were producing wealth, had awakened them. . . . These men were no longer isolated individualists, or libertarians, this is what had changed. . . . The doctrine they claimed to profess, even if the majority of them still were ignorant of its dialectic and precise structure, established a definite relationship between giving and receiving, between energy expended and empty stomachs, between the exploited, they were saying, and the exploiters. (pp. 170–71)

The idea of progress, then, measured in terms of the workers' increasingly sharp consciousness of their rights and interests, and willingness to fight for those rights and interests, lies at the very core of the novel's meaning.

The fact that Metello's father had been an anarchist also has an important meaning in the context of the educative process described in the novel. The picture that emerges from Pratolini's description of the Florentine anarchists is this: they were extraordinary men, full of animal spirits, pugnacious, generous, independent, and above all savagely antagonistic to any and all forms of authority. They were men of heroic proportions. Now Metello is an average man of normal proportions and a typical representative of the new Socialist generation of workers. It is a premise of the novel that Metello's way of thinking, although less colorful than that of his father, nevertheless constitutes the only hope for the mass of exploited workers. The word hope must be emphasized, since Pratolini indicates at various points in the narrative that the extreme rebelliousness of the anarchists was not motivated by genuine confidence in themselves and their cause, but rather by a deep sense of despair and futility. In all of his actions Metello is circumspect and deliberate, while his rash father, Caco, drowned in the Arno because he impetuously ventured into rough waters. Metello learns to control and discipline himself and serves his cause by joining a union and a political party which defend his interests. He acquires the capacity to direct his energies toward concrete and realizable objectives.

Between the day he sets out from Rincine in the summer of 1887 to the spring of 1902, when he assumes a leading role in the strike, Metello goes through a gradual process of development which is conditioned by three factors: the quality of the relationships he establishes with his fellow workers and with the various women in his life, particularly Ersilia; his growing mastery of and devotion to his trade; and finally his acquisition of a general, even if still rudimentary, understanding of the ideas and ideals of socialism.

On the very day he arrives in Florence, weary after a night's walk from Rincine, Metello has an educational experience of capital importance. He accidentally falls in with a group of men loading a vegetable truck. The boss offers him four cents an hour, a wage considerably lower than that earned by the other men. Unaware that by accepting the lower wages he is endangering the bargaining position of the others, Metello immediately starts to work. Later on that day several of his fellow workers warn him in a friendly but decisive tone never to accept lower wages again. This incident occurs in a restaurant in San Frediano. As Metello devours a plate of spaghetti after the day's work is done, he perceives that the men are really of friendly disposition, and quickly concludes that it will be well worth his while to cultivate their esteem:

> Metello ... understood that if he failed to gain the good graces of these men, the police would surely take him back to the farm; and at the same time, it was as if he understood intuitively that only by becoming friends with these men could he achieve permanently the freedom toward which he had walked an entire night. (p. 21)

Thus, it is within the context of everyday, practical experience that the ideas of friendship and interdependence first present themselves to Metello's consciousness.

A year later, practical experience and the timely counsel of a friend once again teach Metello a valuable lesson in social morality. Betto, his surrogate father and intellectual mentor, suddenly disappears. Metello goes to the police station to inquire about the whereabouts of his protector, and immediately arouses the suspicions of the police inspector, since Betto is known as an habitual drunkard and confirmed anarchist. Just for safe measure, the police throw Metello into prison for two days, where he becomes a "real Italian and a real man," since "even before being listed in the register of the Commune, he found himself registered in the lists of the Police." (p. 26) On the night of the first day, he and his fellow inmates are taken to another prison, known as the "murate":

> At nightfall they came to take them to the prison, and it was in this way that for the first time Metello saw a group of men tied to a single chain. (p. 31)

On the second day he is befriended by a young man named Sante Chellini, who first introduces him to the ideas of socialism and from whom he first hears the names Costa and Turati. Because of his own violent temper, which had landed him in jail, Chellini is all the more aware of how important prudence and self-discipline are for a working man. He tells Metello that "the important thing is not to allow oneself to become involved in personal disputes." (p. 33) The chain, at once a symbol of oppression and of the common destiny of men for whom solidarity is a fundamental necessity, becomes associated in Metello's mind with the ideas of socialism, which Chellini tells him can unlock the chain while preserving solidarity.

At the age of twenty, due to the influence of Chellini, of some of his fellow workers, and in particular of Sebastiano Del Buono, Metello rejects the anarchistic ideas of his father and Betto, and enters the ranks of the Socialists. But he does not yet feel ready to join the Socialist party, or to assume any primary responsibilities in the workers' movement. The motto he adopts as a guiding principle at this stage of his career is "never to be the first to move forward nor the last to retreat." (p. 36) In the course of the years, as he acquires knowledge and experience, he will learn to reject this motto, for he will see that at crucial moments of decision, when questions of bread and freedom are involved, circumstances will compel him to move to the forefront of the common struggle for human dignity in which he is engaged.

But Pratolini does not describe Metello's education only in terms of his career as a Socialist and as a worker. Of equal importance to his development is the relationship he establishes with his wife Ersilia. Before meeting Ersilia in 1897, Metello has a whole series of amatory adventures, none of which makes any lasting impression on him. It is apparent that Pratolini stresses the superficial nature of his liaisons with these various women for the purpose of pointing up the significance of his marriage with Ersilia.

The circumstances of the meeting and courtship of Metello and Ersilia are indicative of the central significance that Pratolini attributes to their relationship. Their first meeting occurs at the funeral of Ersilia's father, Quinto, in November, 1897. They see each other rarely in the following months, but it is during this period that we gain an initial insight into Ersilia's character. She is at this time engaged to her employer, a man named Roini, who takes a fancy to her because of her good looks and mastery of her trade, the making of artificial flowers for women's hats. One day, as they are walking together down one of the main thoroughfares in Florence, a crowd of women appears shouting "subversive" slogans and protesting against the unsanitary working conditions in the cigarette manufacturing plant where they work. At the head of the crowd, carrying a banner, is a young girl named Miranda, a friend of Ersilia. Roini declares that the women ought to be led to the gallows. Ersilia turns on him and replies: "That's not true ... they're right." (p. 123) Roini attempts to lead her away, but Ersilia refuses to go with him. Impulsively she breaks their engagement, saying "a woman born in San Frediano needs a man of a different sort." (p. 124) Ersilia is a woman of San Frediano and, like her counterparts in Le ragazze, is fiery and passionately independent. In May of the following year, when she hears of Metello's arrest as a result of his participation in the "demonstrations of '98," she goes to visit him in jail along with the wives and sweethearts of the other imprisoned men. The guards permit them only to shout to their men from outside the prison walls. Metello correctly interprets Ersilia's visit as an expression of deep faith in him. At that moment he decides that he will marry her.

Ersilia is certainly one of Pratolini's most interesting and fully realized feminine characters. She has the virtues of endurance, wit, vivacity and courage of the Ragazze and, in addition, an abundance of common sense on which Metello relies during his moments of doubt and confusion. During the strike, for example, Metello begins to lose his confidence, and it is clear that without the steady, intelligent support of Ersilia he might easily have abdicated his responsibilities to his comrades. It is precisely because the relationship between Metello and Ersilia is so solidly founded on mutual respect and affection that Metello's adulterous adventure with Ida constitutes such a grave breach of marital trust. His adultery cannot be rationalized as the need to fulfill unsatisfied longings. It is motivated by vanity pure and simple, and by a certain capriciousness for which, under other circumstances as well, Ersilia frequently reproaches him. The essential thematic significance of this adulterous episode lies in the fact that it exemplifies Metello's humanness, his egotism, his susceptibility to temptation and error. It is useful to recall in this connection Pratolini's belief that realism "excludes all forms of hagiography." Metello is a stalwart Socialist, and a generally prudent man, but he is no saint.

But a basic question presents itself at this point: how convincingly does Pratolini develop the theme of Metello's education? An objective examination of the text reveals in fact that the force of this theme is severely attenuated by several factors: Pratolini is never quite sure when Metello is acting in accordance with convictions acquired through experience and reflection, and when he is merely following his instincts. In many instances Metello is described as a man who possesses a certain inborn common sense which automatically provides him with the answers to life's problems. As a consequence, the concept of "nature" often seems to overshadow completely that of "education." Metello's development is frequently taken for granted rather than demonstrated. For example, one of the main conflicts in Metello's mind has to do with the question of anarchism versus socialism. Both doctrines appeal to him, the first because it is colorful and anti-legalitarian, the second because it teaches equality and social justice. He chooses socialism, but the motives underlying this choice are not explored. His transition to socialism is described as happening "naturally," because Socialist ideas "appealed to him more."

Viola, one of Metellos' many amatory conquests, tries to spoil him with little gifts, offers of money, and so on. He soon grows weary of being treated like a spoiled child and breaks his liaison with her. This is Pratolini's description of Metello's state of mind just after he had bid permanent farewell to Viola:

> While he was leaving the Cafe to look for work which on that day he was not to find, Viola had already disappeared from his thoughts; she had again and forever become a part of the past which Metello, like all men who are simple and healthy, and who spontaneously adapt themselves to reality, neither asked to relive nor that it in some way be of assistance to him. (p. 80)

That Metello is fundamentally "simple" and "healthy" is an acceptable assumption, but that he has the power to "spontaneously adapt himself to reality," that he is endowed by nature with the ability to grasp reality, seems to stand in direct contradiction with the themes of education and development.

As previously stated, it is a basic premise of *Metello* that genuine progress can be achieved through the collective action of men united by a common purpose and common density. In order to render this idea in concrete terms, Pratolini devotes a large portion of the novel to showing what forces of both unity and dissension were operating within the world of the workers themselves, and to exploring the workers' conflicts with their avowed enemies, principally the capitalists (Badolati) and the reactionary arms of established governmental authority: the police and the army. Also included in Pratolini's picture of Metello's world are two Socialist intellectuals, Del Buono and Pescetti, whose function is to provide the workers with ideological sustenance for their struggles.

The world of the workers is rendered for the most part in a series of scenes of mass meetings, the most important of which are the meeting at Monterivecchi described in chapter twelve, at which the men vote unanimously to go on strike, and the conclave at Fortezza da Basso described in chapter twenty-one, during which discord breaks out between the *oltranzisti* and those who wish to capitulate to the bosses. These two scenes are preceded by discussions and disputes of a more private character between diverse elements within the workers' ranks. The central issue debated by the workers before the strike revolves around the conflict between anarchism and socialism. Most of the older men, who belong to the generation which had come to maturity in the 1860's and 1870's, are more or less of anarchistic persuasion, while the men of Metello's generation tend to favor socialism. The older men stand for rugged individualism and violent rebellion. The Socialists advocate legal reform, collective bargaining, organized demonstrations, and the strike.

The description of the meeting at Monterivecchi gives what appears to be a very accurate picture of the milieu in which Metello moves. The dialogue has an authentic ring, and one can almost hear the sing-song cadence which is so typical of Florentine speech. Here Pratolini's intimate familiarity with the modes of expression, the flavor and tone of the Florentine spoken language served him well indeed. One notes also that the opinions and feelings expressed by each man stem directly from daily experience, and that Pratolini brings us into immediate contact with the inward content, the essence of this experience. The thematic function of these disputes, mass meetings, and outbreaks of violence is of course to illustrate the decisive clash of interests that took place in Florence at the turn of the century between the workers and the bosses, between the burgeoning forces of socialism and the entrenched power of capitalism. Here in Florence, Pratolini is saying, history was being made. Italian society, after the struggle for unity and independence, was entering a new phase of its development, a phase characterized by just such events as those which are described in *Metello*.

But a question similar to the one posed previously regarding the theme of education presents itself: does Pratolini illustrate and develop his thesis in a convincing manner? Is this historic clash of interests powerfully demonstrated? As already noted, the workers' milieu is effectively rendered. It must be said, however, that the other segments and classes of Metello's world are inadequately treated. Capitalism has its spokesman in the figure of Metello's employer Badolati. But there is not one character in the novel, who brings the position and point of view of the government, the monarchy, and the church into clear focus. What remains, therefore, is capitalism, the economic system against which Metello and his comrades are struggling. Capitalism, in *Metello*, is Badolati.

Badolati is repeatedly described by Pratolini as "the best of the worst," the most considerate and sympathetic (in both the Italian and English senses of the word) type of his class. In the vernacular of the workers, he is "the best of the cutthroats." Far from being an unscrupulous and selfish man, he is actively interested in the welfare of his employees. No objection on either philosophical or literary grounds can be raised against a capitalist sympathetically portrayed in a "proletarian" novel. Just as Metello, the stalwart Socialist worker, has his flaws, so Badolati, the capitalist entrepreneur, has his good points. Badolati's genuine warmheartedness can be accepted, but does he appear as a believable representative of a class which, after all, is presumably bent on exploiting the workers? Very probably Pratolini means to suggest that it is precisely because Badolati is benevolently paternalistic that he is so dangerous. He lulls the workers into thinking that he has their best interests at heart, while in reality he is just as vigorous an exponent of the capitalist system as the most pitiless sweatshop proprietor. But in order to convince us of this, Badolati would also have to have his cynical, hypocritical side. He is neither a cynic nor a hypocrite. He remains throughout an honest, hardworking man who wants to do everything possible for his employees.

Pratolini's portrayals of the Socialist intellectuals Del Buono and Pescetti leave much to be desired in terms of his own conception of what constitutes realistic delineation of character. According to his own definition, the realist must be able "to synthesize in the characters of his novel all the characteristic and typical elements of the class or society to which they belong." Instead of emphasizing their function as intellectuals and Socialist ideologists, Pratolini dresses them in the mythical garb of modern folk heroes. The "legendary" aura that surrounds both Del Buono and Pescetti seems out of place in a novel whose characters and plot are designed presumably to give the reader a realistic understanding of a period in Italian history. As an historical novel, *Metello* is not entirely successful, since only rarely does one sense a profoundly causal link between the historical events and persons referred to and the incidents in Florence.

There is an explanation for the relative unimportance and extrinsicality of these references to contemporary political events and figures. It lies in an assumption that Pratolini makes about Metello and his comrades, namely that it was not so much their intelligence, their ideas, their moral convictions that inspired them to struggle for their rights as it was their "instinct," their "natural force":

> It was their instinct more than their intelligence that enlightened them; a brutal but explicit truth consoled them with its rightness. And more even than their leaders, who tended to be quickly dispersed or to deviate from former positions, even if they almost always paid personally for what they believed, it was their own natural force that guided these people straight on their path. (p. 171)

If the Florentine workers were guided mainly by their "natural force," it follows that the influence of Costa, Turati, and the other Socialist leaders of the time could not have been decisive.

In the speech he delivered to a Congress of Construction Workers in January, 1956, Pratolini made reference to the stormy literary controversy that had been stirred by *Metello*. "I do not want to adopt the air of one who accepts praise and refuses criticism," he said. "I know only too well that *Metello* is a still imperfect work." But, he added, what is new and correct and successful is my effort to make a place at long last in our literature for characters who represent the ever more vital and pressing reality of the world of labor; characters of the working class who are portrayed neither demagogically, nor in a falsely condescending manner, nor from an abstract and insanely sanguinary point of view.

Now there can be no doubt that *Metello* does fulfill the purposes to which Pratolini alludes in the statement quoted above. There is no trace of demagoguery in the novel, nor does Pratolini err either on the side of condescension or of "sanguinary" partisanship in his depiction of the world of labor. He focuses his attention consistently on the concrete life problems of his characters.

As he himself recognizes, however, *Metello* "is a still imperfect work." With respect to the central theme of education, it is evident that Pratolini was working at cross purposes. On the one hand, he intended to describe the gradual process of development by virtue of which Metello (and in a broader sense the entire Italian working-class movement) acquired an awareness of his own identity as a worker, as a Socialist, and as a man with commitments and responsibilities. Yet on the other hand, as evidenced by certain of the passages quoted in our discussion of the novel, he conceived of Metello as a person fundamentally and "spontaneously adapted to reality" whose belief in the dignity of labor, human solidarity, and socialism itself derived above all from the "natural" condition of life in which he found himself. The same is true of Pratolini's conception of the workers as a whole. In his description of the workers' struggles, Pratolini relied for the most part on the same formulas that guided him in *Il Quartiere*. Such words and phrases as "instinct," "spontaneous," "natural force," the "natural solidarity of the poor," appear frequently in *Metello*, and necessarily attenuate the themes of education and social progress with which the novel is basically concerned.

In the course of his interview with Carlo Bo, Pratolini revealed that he began working on *Lo scialo* [10] in the early part of 1950, about a year and a half before beginning *Metello*. "I had to begin from there," he said, "since it was the material with which I was most familiar. I had to rewrite the *Cronache,* nothing else, but seen from the other side of the barricade." Although it is true that *Lo scialo* deals with many of the same events depicted in *Cronache,* the above-quoted statement must not be taken too literally. As we shall see, *Lo scialo* is much more than a mere rewriting of *Cronache* "seen from the other side of the barricade." In the summer of 1951 Pratolini began writing *Metello.* After the publication of *Metello* in February 1955, he resumed work on *Lo scialo* and by the latter part of 1957 the novel was practically finished. Because of its extraordinary length (1343 pages), it was published by Mondadori in two volumes.

Pratolini describes *Lo scialo* as "the novel of the small and middle bourgeoisie, 1910 to 1930, seen (critically I hope) from within." [11] It takes up approximately where *Metello* left off, but is connected to the first volume of *Una Storia Italiana* only in a temporal sense. It has a completely different cast of characters and, as suggested by the word *scialo,*[12] its central theme and mood are diametrically opposed to those of *Metello.*

Lo scialo comprises seven Books which vary in length from about one hundred to three hundred pages. Book I, entitled *The Vegnis and the Corsinis,* covers the years 1914 to 1921, and deals with the marriage and short-lived happiness of Giovanni Corsini and Nella Vegni. In the spring of 1919, Spartaco Gavagnini, the leader of the Florentine Socialist party, asks Giovanni to run for office on the Socialist ticket. Giovanni accepts, but is defeated in the elections. In 1921 Gavagnini is murdered by the Fascists, several of whom see Giovanni at Gavagnini's funeral and subject him to a savage beating. Consequently, Giovanni decides that he had better abandon politics and pursue a business career, which soon turns out to be based on the buying and selling of stolen scrap iron.

Book II, entitled *The Battignanis and the Maestris,* traces the life of Nini Battignani from 1908 to 1919. In 1913 and 1914 she becomes the "queen" of the Florentine bourgeoisie, whose social and cultural life revolves around two businessmen's clubs. In April, 1915, the two Clubs stage a jointly sponsored Interventionists' Rally. Filled with patriotic ardor, and dressed in the colors of the Italian flag, Nini is the center of attraction at the rally. Soon after the end of the war, Nini's father, now old and sick, tells her that he is in serious financial straits and has only two choices: sell his business, or hand everything over to his assistant Adamo Maestri in the hope that he will rebuild the family fortune. Nini sees that her only hope lies in marrying Adamo, whom she nevertheless despises as a servant unworthy of her attention.

In Book III, entitled *The Bigazzis and the Malescis,* we see the daily life of Giovanni and Nella in 1924 through the eyes of their son Fernando. The technique used here, as in a large portion of the novel, is that of interior monologue broken up by occasional interpretative comments and descriptive passages.

In Book IV, entitled *Nini in 1921, with the Falornis, the Bertinis, the Sangiorgis and the Neris,* we learn of Nini's failure to find happiness with Adamo. She has a nervous collapse and retires to her farm in Vingone. There she becomes involved in a lesbian affair with a peasant girl named Maria.

Book V, entitled *The Corsinis and the Maestris, a New Life,* takes up the life of Giovanni and Nella in 1926. Nella, who has grown more and more alienated from Giovanni, begins an affair with the Fascist Folco Malesci. On the evening of their second rendezvous at Folco's villa, Folco has a violent quarrel with some of his comrades. After the quarrel, Folco becomes restless and he and Nella leave the villa. As they are getting in the car, Folco is shot. The assassin, as we learn later, was Nini. Folco had come to symbolize in her eyes all the destructive impulses which she felt within herself. Less than a year later, in a more conclusive act of self-repudiation, Nini will take her own life.

Book VI, entitled *Erina, Ricimero, and Nella with Her Secret,* first deals with the relationship of Giovanni and his mistress, Erina. Erina persuades him to give her a check of five thousand lire with which, she says, she will buy and resell some waste wool at a handsome profit for both of them. Meanwhile Giovanni's scrap iron business hits a snag. New government regulations forbid further private speculation in this area, but he finds out about this only after he has given his friend Bugatti his ten percent commission. Then Erina cashes his check and leaves town with a travelling variety show. Giovanni is left with a few hundred lire in the bank.

The principal events in Book VII, entitled *The Corsinis, then Nini, on the Same Day, around* 1930, actually take place in 1927. Giovanni's past political activities bring his career to a sudden and pathetic end. Suspected by the police of anti-Fascist beliefs, which of course Giovanni had long since abandoned, he had been followed for several weeks by government secret agents. He is arrested and taken off to prison where, it is suggested, he will remain for many years.

In the concluding pages the scene shifts to Nini's farm in Vingone. Corinna and Simone, a peasant couple, talk at length and with great wisdom about all the events in their lives during the preceding ten years. It is late in the morning. Corinna, growing anxious about Nini, who usually arises much earlier, goes up to her room. She finds Nini dead in the bathtub; "Her eyes were closed; and on her face there was a quietude and a smile that had never been a part of her."

Lo scialo is an exhaustive psychological probing into the motives and feelings of the three principal characters, Giovanni, Nella, and Nini. "Contradiction" is a key word in Pratolini's psychological studies of his three principal characters. Giovanni is in 1919 an ardent Socialist, yet at the very moment when the situation in Florence demands resolute action on his part, he withdraws entirely from politics and involves himself in a dishonest business venture. When Gavagnini asks him to run in the elections of 1919, he tells his wife with customary bravado: "I've always been a Socialist, I have never compromised with my ideas." (p. 32) After he loses the election, he receives a letter of consolation and moral support from Gavagnini. Two years later, immediately after Gavagnini is murdered, Giovanni throws the letter in the incinerator. "Of course I burned it," he thinks to himself, "didn't I have to burn it, after what happened . . . ?" (p. 75) He not only withdraws from political life, but in burning the letter performs a symbolic act of renunciation and cowardice that will torment him for the rest of his days.

It is a premise of *Lo scialo*, as of all of Pratolini's major works, that every individual thought and action, no matter how seemingly inconsequential, forms part of a complex pattern of interdependence from which no person can separate himself. Thus Giovanni's deal with Bugatti produces a painful conflict in the mind of his son, Fernando. Erminio Vegni, Giovanni's father-in-law, is a skilled goldsmith and a man of integrity. Therefore he reacts to Giovanni's request for help in his dishonest business venture with anger and contempt. He is deeply attached to his grandson, but he refuses to sacrifice his principles, even for the sake of remaining on good terms with his family. The break between Erminio and Giovanni is irreparable. Fernando, still too young to understand the issue involved in the quarrel, takes his father's side, but at the same time becomes aware of the contradictory position in which he is now placed: "On the Sunday when the argument took place, he had understood, still instinctively, that in order to hold the affection of his father and mother he would be compelled to deprive himself of his grandfather's love." (p. 295)

In the first chapters of the novel, it becomes immediately apparent that Nella's life too is characterized by a whole host of irreconcilable impulses and aspirations. She is first described as a sensual woman given to "sudden fits of melancholy and equally sudden enthusiasms." At the beginning of her marriage she experiences intense sexual pleasure with Giovanni, yet deeply rooted guilt feelings and inhibitions, complicated by certain vague religious scruples, prevent her from ever achieving a true sense of closeness with him. She has respect for her father, and at best a sentimental affection for Giovanni, whose weakness of character often gives her cause for alarm. Yet she defends Giovanni in his quarrel with her father, saying that unless Giovanni succeeds in his venture,

> "We wouldn't have any further hope of improving our position. Do you know how we'll grow old? This way, surrounded by the pretty misery and mediocrity in which we've always lived. . . ." (p. 109)

Her lack of faith in Giovanni, mistrust of Bugatti, and acute awareness of the precariousness of her situation come into direct conflict with her "desire, now desperately rekindled, for a life of comfort, of worldly pleasures, of privileges serenely enjoyed." (p. 129)

Nini's personality is even more full of contradictions than that of Giovanni and Nella. During her childhood she was pampered and doted on by her parents. Her father, a successful merchant, gave her everything she wanted, including the right to treat persons of lower social station with that mixture of philanthropic concern, imperiousness, and disdain that continues to characterize her attitude toward most people when she becomes a mature woman. She acquires what Pratolini calls the "regal" capacity "to involve herself in the sorrows of the common people and to emerge from them intact" (p. 159), a capacity which later prevents her from achieving a satisfying relationship with her husband, Adamo; for Adamo is of humble origins, and had been, together with the children of the peasant families of Vingone, "one of the first persons with regard to whom Nini had given vent to her natural exuberance, her characteristically philanthropic spirit." (p. 159) By reason of her mother's noble blood, Nini thinks of herself as a "princess" to whom all ordinary mortals must make obeisances. Yet when she does gain entrance into aristocratic circles, she remembers that the real source of her wealth and social position is her thoroughly bourgeois father and declines an invitation to a ball extended to her by the Crown Prince.

But Nini is not really willing to accept the fact that she is an "obscure bourgeoise." After the death of Gioietta Donati, who had been responsible for her acceptance by the Florentine nobility, Nini becomes morose, for she realizes that without Gioietta's help she will in fact be an "obscure bourgeoise." This she fears more than anything else. Then her impossible love for the aristocrat Guido Donati precipitates another in the series of emotional crises which mark every stage of her career. Guido is a homosexual without the slightest interest in women. Yet Nini deludes herself into thinking that he worships her from afar. His aloofness infuriates her:

> The will, at once stubborn and virile, with which Nini was endowed, her vivacity and restlessness, her anxious attachment to life, would never be strong enough to obliterate the bitterness she felt at seeing herself ... rejected by the man to whom she had promised herself. (p. 169)

Another dominant psychological characteristic of Giovanni, Nella, and Nini is their tendency, which becomes more and more pronounced as the years pass, to evaluate themselves and others exclusively in terms of social status. Their self-esteem rises and falls in accordance with the degree of acceptance they receive from the class of people to which they aspire to belong. For Giovanni and Nella, it is acceptance by the prosperous group of merchants, professional men and government officials who gravitate around the two businessmen's clubs which represents the fulfillment of all their dreams. Nini takes the amenities and privileges of her bourgeois existence for granted, so that her goal is to move in aristocratic circles.

Giovanni feels a sense of boundless gratitude to Nini, whose friendship with Nella allowed him to gain entry into the businessmen's club. And gratitude to someone of higher social station, as always in Giovanni's case, is inextricably bound up with contempt for the same "factory people" whose rights and interests he had once held sacred as a Socialist. Giovanni is not a cruel man, nor is he infected with the lust for violence and power that typifies the hard core Fascists portrayed in the novel. Yet that Nini is on close terms with Folco Malesci, one of the men who murdered his benefactor Gavagnini, and that many of the leading personalities at the club have become prominent figures in the Fascist movement, only serves to intensify his admiration for her.

Nella's ruling passion is to live a life of luxury and ease. She does not find it too difficult to reconcile herself to Giovanni's lack of moral rectitude, "since honesty and righteousness had not been able to elevate even minimally her social position." (p. 129) She, too, feels irresistibly attracted to the world of the powerful and the prosperous. In the glitter of the bourgeois milieu to which Nini introduces her, she finds "her natural fulfillment." Toward the end of Book V, ironically entitled *The Corsinis and the Maestris, a New Life*, when Giovanni and Nella reach the pinnacle of social success, from which they will soon fall as a result of the lies and contradictions on which their life together is based, Nella is no longer preoccupied at all by the moral compunctions she had felt at the outset of Giovanni's career in the scrap iron business:

She had by now ceased considering Giovanni's actions; it was of no importance whether his partnership with Bugatti was clean or dishonest: the comfort, the "new life" that Giovanni had achieved was enough for her. (p. 828)

Nini's craving for high social position is also accompanied by a correspondingly intense loathing for people of the working class. Her feelings in this respect closely resemble those of Nella, and are illustrated most clearly in her contemptuous attitude toward the workers' "demonstrations of '98," which she remembers witnessing at the age of ten. The "demonstrations of '98," in *Metello*, symbolize the revolutionary dawn of the Italian working-class movement, but in *Lo scialo*, seen "from the other side of the barricade," from the point of view of Nini and her class, they become naturally a cause for consternation and alarm.

The contradictions, hypocrisies, and craving for social success which characterize the lives of Giovanni, Nella, and Nini reflect the gnawing sense of inner emptiness that constitutes a basic element of their personalities. This sense of emptiness manifests itself in the trivial amusements with which they while away their time, in their gossipiness and exaggerated preoccupation with other people's opinion of them, in their flight from responsibility and boredom, in their endless and impossible pursuit of happiness outside themselves.

To relieve the tortured emptiness of his life, Giovanni develops a morbid fascination with the stories of crime and violence that appear more and more frequently in the daily newspaper. Virtually everything Giovanni does has a tawdry, flimsy quality. First he deals in scrap iron. Then, through his mistress Erina, whose coarseness attracts him, he hopes to make a big profit on the resale of waste wool. Bereft of resources after the failure of his scrap iron business and betrayal by Erina, he turns in despair to the Fascist Leandro Neri for assistance. Neri gives him an equivocal answer. He returns to his store and ruminates:

He took the chair, placed it in the center of the store, "in the middle of nothing," and sat down. He felt the darkness around and behind him; in front there was the strip of road framed by the entrance through which, when the street was empty, one could see "a naked wall," there was a cat curled up on the sidewalk. "Aren't you the lucky cat," he sighed, "in one way or the other you'll always find a scrap of food; you don't have to be recommended or be grateful to anyone, if you're in the mood you trail a female, you grab her by the neck and then slip it in ... and I'm here," he said shaking himself, "dead tired, with a splitting headache, my chest feels like it's on fire, imagining the strangest things." (p. 1271)

In Nella's case, inner emptiness assumes a somewhat different psychological form. She tries to compensate for the void within her first by relying on the ritual of confession and then, when that fails to bring her the solace she desires, by adopting a completely fatalistic conception of life. The reason for her unhappiness, she concludes, does not lie within her, but rather in a predetermined pattern of events over which neither she nor anyone else can exercise control. With her marriage "reduced to external gestures, and on her part to constant hypocrisy" (p. 939), and having suffered the torments of the damned after the murder of her lover Folco Malesci, it is natural that she should escape into fatalism:

> Now she told herself that life is this incessant succession of cruelties: a waste, an indiscriminate squandering of fatal shocks like the tremors of an earthquake, under whose wreckage creatures of her sort, weak, dominated, capable only of devotion, are inevitably buried. (p. 944)

Because of her sophistication, intelligence, and especially her often brutal frankness with herself and others, Nini has the ability to recognize that the source of her difficulties lies within herself. The causes of her unhappiness and constant feeling of emptiness remain for the most part unknown to her, but she does make an important admission to herself, after she has decided to marry Adamo and re-enter the social whirl:

> There is something rotten in you, Nini, that cannot be cured. And the time has come for you to resign yourself, there's no way out of it. This is your condition." (p. 290)

As a social novel, *Lo scialo* is concerned primarily with the small and middle bourgeoisie, since it was this segment of society that, in Pratolini's opinion, assumed the role of protagonist of this juncture of Italian history and that "formed . . . the cowardly but stubborn, obtuse, timorous, calumnious army behind whose domestic bayonets fascism established itself.[13] The first significant reference the Florentine bourgeoisie appears at the beginning of the second part of Book II, where we learn that between the war in Tripoli in 1912 and the outbreak of the first World War, this class elected none other than Nini Battignani as its "private queen." From what we have already learned about Nini in the preceding pages—her imperiousness, her contempt for people of lower social station, her aversion to men, her inability to find significant life objectives for herself—the fact that she scores such an immediate success among the men and women of the club suggests that they are not entirely immune from the "something rotten," the *scialo* of triviality, deceit and corruption with which the novel is concerned.

Nini devotes herself assiduously to the cultural, social, and philanthropic activities which constitute the club's reason for being. She also assumes the role of matchmaker on behalf of her many girl friends, for whom virginity is the highest virtue and marriage with a man of property the dominant, indeed the exclusive, concern:

> The young girls had immediately thrown themselves into her arms; and with even greater reason after having learned of her adventure with the Count of Turin: expert judges of her lack of good looks, and educated to consider virginity as the major and decisively important virtue, they never regarded Nini as a rival. Next to a woman who had moved in high society, who was a skilled rider and a treasure of refined manners, who had enjoyed the attentions and caresses of a Savoy, they had everything to learn and nothing to fear. Instinctively, the not so little foxes understood that to place themselves at Nini's side, to be dominated temporarily by her, meant not to become less, but rather to gain in value in the eyes of their various "prospects." (p. 192)

In the next scene, we see Nini and her circle gathered together at a great Interventionists' Rally. Certain quarrels of a private nature which had thus far caused some discord are now forgotten. This event re-establishes a perfect unity of feeling and purpose among the members. Even the tender young virgins who gasp with terror at the mere mention of the words "proletariat," "revolution," and "socialism," find themselves joining in spontaneously with the chorus of voices, singing:

> "Without pity we'll ram our bayonets
> into the backs of those dogs."

Nini, dressed in the colors of the Italian flag, is the sensation of the evening.

After the war, Nini retains for a while her status as "queen" of the Florentine bourgeoisie, but now seated next to her in a still loftier position are two men: Guido Donati, aristocrat, war hero, and African colonizer who has been honored with the title of President of the Boatmen's Club, and Folco Malesci, heir to his father's construction company, flying ace, and founder of the first Florentine *Fascio*. It is at this point that we see the cult of the hero, what Pratolini has called the bourgeois' "inextinguishable devotion to the strong," manifest itself with unmistakable clarity. A mystique of hero worship surrounds the figure of Donati at the Boatmen's Club:

> He had only to cross the bridge to go from his rooms in the Donati palace to the Boatmen's Club. There everyone hung on his every word, although within proper bounds he was also opposed from time to time. Just as the kitten stretches out its paw towards the patient wolfhound, some people occasionally beat him at the betting table, others allowed themselves to question his preference for Martell in comparison with Armagnac and Courvoisier.
>
> "He's loaded with property, glory, and prestige," they said, usually close enough to him so that he could hear them.
>
> "Without counting the special property grants he has in Somalia. They're so vast they stretch from . . . help me, from . . ."
>
> The members of the Boatmen's Club were not strong in geography. (p. 251)

Folco Malesci is also held in the highest esteem by the ladies who congregate each afternoon at Doney's Cafe:

"He's becoming a bigshot."

"But he's always been one."

"D'Annunzio has written to him."

"Mussolini has called him on the telephone."

"The police chief wants to talk to him." (p. 256)

The aristocracy is only very briefly portrayed in the first and third parts of Book two, and there can be no doubt that with these two scenes Pratolini intended merely to suggest the irreparable decadence of the Florentine nobility during the historical period concerned. The aristocracy is represented chiefly by the Donati family, composed of the Marchese and Contessa Donati, and their two children, Guido and Gioietta. In view of the fact that in *Lo scialo* Pratolini aims to describe the life of an historical epoch in terms of its dominant social and political trends, it is apparent that he could not but emphasize the decline of a social stratum that had long since lost its vitality and its reason for being. The scene describing the funeral of the Contessa Laura Donati, a woman greatly admired by her aristocratic friends for her long and useful life devoted to philanthropic work on behalf of *il popolino*, is clearly intended to serve a symbolic function:

> Her hands folded on her bosom, holding a crown, stood out on the dark blue brocade, trimmed with lace, in which they had dressed her. There was something gently ironic and contented in the expression of her closed lips, in her slumberer's surrender. One might have said that she wished to communicate to those who remained behind the pleasure she felt in the journey she had just undertaken, almost an invitation. (p. 239)

As already noted, *Lo scialo* is the first work of Pratolini in which characters belonging to the working class are not the protagonists. The reason for this lies in Pratolini's historical analysis of the period treated in the novel, a period during which "the evolution and struggles, the authentic and obscure heroism" of the working-class movement "culminated in a terrible defeat." [14] It is true, of course, that in *Cronache* he dealt with essentially the same period described in *Lo scialo*, and that the protagonists of the earlier work were proletarians. The difference between the two works lies in the fact that *Cronache* was intended to be a picture of proletarian life under Fascist domination, while *Lo scialo* was written from an historical point of view, and reflects Pratolini's objective analysis of the period. Consequently, he devotes relatively little attention to the working class in *Lo scialo*.

The novel does however contain a number of splendid scenes depicting the Florentine workers en masse. It contains in addition a group of minor characters, the Bigazzi family, who are intended to typify the moral and political attitudes of a segment of the Florentine working class during the early years of the Fascist epoch. The Bigazzis live in an apartment directly beneath that of Giovanni and Nella in Santa Croce. The relationship between the two families is at first friendly, but when Mario Bigazzi discovers that Giovanni has never told his son Fernando that he (Giovanni) was at one time a railroad worker, he begins to suspect his friend of a certain hypocrisy. But the real crisis in the relationship between the Corsinis and the Bigazzis occurs when Nella inadvertently reveals to Libero Bigazzi that she and Giovanni have been consorting with Folco Malesci at the businessmen's club. The bitter quarrel which ensues emphasizes the opposed values of the two families and, it is suggested, of the worlds in which they move. Giovanni, despite his democratic pretensions, cannot help but admire Folco, since he worships power, no matter what form it assumes or for what purposes it is used. For Mario, on the other hand, Folco is "the hangman of the Pignone," the organizer of Fascist punitive expeditions which threaten to destroy the solidarity and power of resistance of the working class.

There is still a fourth social stratum depicted in *Lo scialo*, that of the peasant families of Vingone, the Bertinis and the Falornis. But in view of the fact that we see the peasants' world almost entirely through the eyes of Nini, and since Pratolini's description of their struggles is so closely bound up with his treatment of the theme of fascism, it is necessary now to examine this theme in its principal forms and ramifications. With respect to the theme of fascism in *Lo scialo*, it is important to keep in mind a statement Pratolini made to Carlo Bo regarding all three volumes of *Una Storia Italiana*, namely that he had chosen to render the social and political events of each period "through the private experiences of the characters." In *Lo scialo* fascism is treated of course on one level as an objective political phenomenon. There are a number of scenes, such as the battle between the Fascist squadrists and the workers of the Pignone described in the second part of Book III, which do not directly reflect or involve the private feelings and motives of the characters. This scene, based on an event which actually took place in Florence in 1921, as well as many passages of straight expository writing interspersed throughout the novel, are designed to lend a sense of historical reality to the narrative, and they fulfill this function very well indeed. What must be stressed, however, is that Pratolini does not treat fascism primarily as an objective political phenomenon, as an "event" in Italian history. On the contrary, he is concerned more fundamentally with its moral and psychological impact on the lives of his characters.

Of basic importance therefore are the feelings and attitudes regarding fascism of the novel's three main characters, Giovanni, Nella, and Nini. In 1919, Giovanni identifies himself with the reformist Socialists headed in the Italian parliament by Turati. As a consequence, he opposes the radical nationalists who have gravitated around Mussolini. The murder of Spartaco Gavagnini in the spring of 1921 begins a reign of terror in Florence. A genuine feeling of grief at Gavagnini's death makes Giovanni attend his funeral, an act for which he pays a heavy price. Several days after the funeral he is suddenly attacked by a group of blackshirts, who scream foul curses at him as they pour castor oil down his throat. For a man of Giovanni's fundamentally passive, nonviolent disposition, this is a terrifying experience. From that point on Giovanni's prime motive is to make quick and easy profit in his scrap iron business. Yet it is significant that he never succeeds completely in forgetting his friendship with Gavagnini, or in suppressing the resentment he feels because he is compelled to look upon every person he meets as a potential spy or informer. On the afternoon of the day in 1927 when he is arrested he finds himself standing on a familiar corner of the city. He suddenly notices two memorial tablets, one to Collodi, the other to Cellini, which had never attracted his attention before. Through a natural association of ideas, he thinks of Spartaco Gavagnini, for whom no memorial has ever been erected. "A piece of stone that might remind us of Spartaco, that they still have to dig out: but his name is written in our hearts," —the private testimony of a decent, albeit a cowardly and conformist man who is caught up in and overwhelmed by the terror that surrounds him.

Nella's emotional responses to the heroes of the new Fascist order reveal another characteristic of the type of mentality to which Pratolini ascribes the growth and triumph of fascism. One of Nella's weaknesses is her tendency, which becomes increasingly pronounced and detached from all moral considerations, to idolize "strong men." The amoral nature of her responses to strong men becomes plainly evident when she develops an irresistible desire to make love with Folco Malesci. Nini, who is sexually interested in Nella, tries to warn her against getting involved with Folco, and catalogs his crimes in a convincing manner. But Nini's warning, instead of dissuading Nella from seeing Folco, only serves to heighten his fascination for her. Given the fact of Nella's "inextinguishable devotion to the strong," one of the salient features of her personality, it is inevitable that she should find in Folco the embodiment of her dreams for social success and prestige.

Before discussing the nature of Nini's involvement with fascism, it will be useful to examine the attitudes expressed by five of the other characters with whom she is in close personal contact: her husband Adamo, her doctor Alessandro, her friend Imelde Salimbeni, Guido Donati, and Folco Malesci. Although he sympathizes with the idea of democratic socialism and contributes money to the besieged peasants of Scandicci, Adamo's point of view is best exemplified in a scene which depicts him, his assistant Franco, and Nini talking together in the back room of his warehouse. Nini asks Franco what his political beliefs are. Franco answers for himself and for Adamo:

"If I have to be sincere, I'll admit that I don't have any precise opinion. Adamo doesn't have any precise ideas

either; isn't that right, Adamo, except with regard to business, a precise idea?" (p. 413)

It is a measure of his goodness that Adamo lends a helping
hand to the peasants, but it is also a measure of his failure
that he has no "precise idea" as to what fascism is.

Nini's doctor, Alessandro, with whom she forms a
momentarily satisfying intellectual relationship, typifies
the point of view of Italy's liberal intelligentsia. A man
of literary interests and humanitarian sentiments, Alessandro sees fascism for exactly what it is, yet he is incapable
of meeting its challenge except with abstract ideas derived from his reading of the liberal French and English
philosophers. He speaks eloquently in the name of en-
lightenment, social progress, and the perfectibility of man-
kind. But although Alessandro finds it impossible to determine a firm course of action, he puts his finger on one of
the prime causes of fascism, namely the willingness of the
powerful landowners and industrialists to use the young
Fascist "thugs" as instruments with which to protect
their economic interests against the peasantry and the
urban proletariat:

> "Their liberalism is everything ignorant people imagine
> the Middle Ages to have been: it's obscurantism, it's in-
> quisition, even and above all if they're masons. The war?
> But the war for them was only an episode. Now they're
> trying to dominate the scene with these young thugs. . . .
> And as far as the thugs themselves are concerned, they're
> tools, they aren't worth the contempt that is usually re-
> served for the *maquereaux*. That's the level. They are little
> D'Annunzios who lack genius." (pp. 582–83)

From Imelde Salimbeni, the daughter of one of Tuscany's most powerful landowners, we get still another point
of view toward fascism. She attempts to persuade Nini
to contribute money to Fascist headquarters in Scandicci
since, she says, the Fascists are the only people left in
Italy who can protect the rights of property. Speaking of
the workers and farmers of Tuscany, Imelde says:

> "around here they've formed certain cooperatives, certain
> leagues, certain societies, as they call them, and meeting
> places for their parties, labor unions; to make a long story

short, a whole network of organizations intent on subverting the law and the rights of property. Do I make myself clear?" (p. 559)

Guido Donati's judgment of fascism undergoes a marked change. At first, like Alessandro, during the early 1920's, he makes an accurate analysis of Mussolini and of the Fascist mentality. But only several years later, after his return to Somalia as explorer and colonizer, Guido sends a long letter to Nini in which he reveals a radical change of opinion with respect to Mussolini and fascism:

> "Every letter and newspaper we receive serves to reconfirm it, and I confess to you that I observe with admiration how Mussolini is assuming a stature that even a few years ago would have still been impossible to imagine. Perhaps his movement is the only one capable of restoring the order on which freedom must sustain itself, in a country destined otherwise to be governed by mob rule." (p. 469)

Among the hard core Fascists portrayed in *Lo scialo*, Folco Malesci is undoubtedly the most idealistic, if such a word can be applied to a man who believes so deeply in the mystique of conquest and power. The difference is minimal, perhaps, but it exists. It lies primarily in the fact that Folco, according to Pratolini's interpretation, is a "Florentine" Fascist, a *uomo di parte*, in short, a man for whom the world is divided into "friends and enemies." Hence in the early years of the Fascist epoch he led his "faction" into battle against enemies he genuinely hated. In Folco's case one cannot quite speak of violence for the sake of violence.

As for Nini's involvement in fascism, the key word to describe her feelings is "ambivalence." She is at once attracted to and repelled by men of Folco's type. She first becomes involved in fascism immediately after the war, when out of a patriotic impulse unaccompanied by rational reflection she sends a letter of endorsement, cosigned by Folco and bearing the heading "Florentine Businessmen's Club," to the newly formed *Fasci di Combattimento* in Milan. When the letter is published in the newspaper *Il Popolo d'Italia*, the leaders of the Club call a special meeting and vote to censure Nini and Folco, since "the Club, by reason of its apolitical character and

essentially social purpose, cannot become involved in political positions, 'sacrosanct, but private.'" (p. 220) Nini
reacts to this by calling the President of the Club a
"profiteer," a "vampire," and a "slob," and promptly
withdraws her membership. In this instance Nini's attitude probably typifies that of many young Italians during
the immediate postwar years. She is offended by the
"business and pleasure as usual" state of mind which
characterizes the club. She cannot accept the fact that,
despite the sacrifices of the Italian people, small groups
of profiteers, *pescecani*, are carrying on their activities as
if nothing had changed in Italy. The *Fasci* represent for
her the continuation of that spirit of national pride and
militance which had originally led her country to take
sides in the war. On a point of honor, she joins the
Florentine *Fascio*, but again more out of impulse than a
genuine sense of commitment. For Nini is not really
interested in politics. Her enthusiasm for all types of
causes tends to increase or wane in accordance with her
moods, which in turn vary from euphoria to extreme melancholy, depending on the responses of the man or woman
in whom she is interested at the moment.

But it is in the latter part of 1920 and the early months
of 1921 that Nini's ambivalent attitude manifests itself
most dramatically. As already noted, Nini is also sexually
ambivalent, in that, although she is attracted to certain
types of men, the deepest and most instinctive part of
her nature craves intimacy with persons of her own sex.
Intercourse with Adamo had proved to be "a torment,"
so that escape to Vingone had become an imperious necessity. She has an intensely exciting affair with her servant
Maria, and for a few months at Vingone she feels certain that her life has at long last assumed a definitive
pattern. Then a "series of circumstances" crushes her short-
lived happiness. Maria turns out to be a nymphomaniac
and, as we learn later, a spy in the service of Leandro
Neri, who had paid her to report on the "subversive"
activities of the Falornis and the Bertinis. Then Nini begins to suspect that her peasants are plotting to destroy
her. Actually the peasants still respect her, but in view
of the Fascists' punitive expeditions against them they
insist that she either choose to remain at Vingone and

fight on their side or return to Florence. Bixio Falorni makes the peasants' position very clear to Nini. Lorina Falorni, Bixio's wife and the schoolteacher of Scandicci, explains to Nini why so many of her peasants have become Communists:

"Those soldiers have put up a sign. On it was written: COMMUNISTS SURRENDER! THE FIRING SQUAD AWAITS YOU. Our men shot it down. They responded with the same sign. Later they put up another one: THE COMMUNISTS ARE RUINING YOU. LEAVE THEM ALONE. That would be tantamount to saying: Scandicci, rid yourself of everyone. Communism is in our blood, reasons come later. What it is doesn't require much effort for people who labor to know, who are subjugated, who have always endured repression: it's the socialism of those who really want socialism, say these fellows. Then Bixio, Arduino Bertini, me from time to time, those who know more than the three of us, convince them with ideas." (p. 682)

Nini finds it impossible to take a position. On the one hand, she still admires Folco for his daring and his superior intelligence. She also owes a debt of gratitude to the squadrists for having defended her property rights against the wave of collectivism which swept over Italy after the war. On the other hand, she is horrified by the Fascists' cruelty, and wishes to protect her peasants from physical harm. But she has grown alienated from the two families because they are no longer willing to accept her brand of paternalism, and want to take their lives into their own hands. Nini remains permanently perplexed. After several of the Falornis are killed, she abandons Vingone in despair, still undecided, tormented, irresolute. As she prepares to return to Florence, she can only mutter to herself:

"They're the same, Maria, as you say: equal. Bixio, and Gigi and Carlo whom you'd like to save, no different from Sangiorgi and Neri. Like Folco! Like the doctor: oh I don't know...." (p. 676)

Thus, because of her inability to take a position even during moments of grave crisis, Nini is swept up by the tide of events that runs inexorably towards fascism.

The triumph of fascism, then, is described from many different angles and points of view in *Lo scialo*. Giovanni's passivity and cowardice, Nini's ambivalence, Nella's adoration of "strong men," the ill-fated resistance of the peasants of Vingone, Folco's cult of the superman, Guido's complacency, and the feelings and attitudes of the scores of other characters who appear in the narrative serve to elucidate the ways in which the *scialo* of deceit and cruelty embodied in fascism extended its influence into every segment of Florentine society.

EPILOGUE

BOTH *Metello* and *Lo scialo* are "private stories" that take place within the context of Italian society during the years 1870 to 1930. These two novels, like the third volume of *Una Storia Italiana* which is to appear shortly, are based on the experiences of individuals whose life patterns are to a large extent "typical" of entire social strata. The story of Metello Salani is broadly speaking also the story of the Italian working class "at its revolutionary dawn." Giovanni, Nella and Nini are representative of the *petite bourgeoisie* at the beginning of the Fascist era. It is through the depiction of these characters portrayed in their social milieu that Pratolini has sought to provide what he has called "a truthful picture of the life and society of our time."

In the early part of 1962, Pratolini temporarily set aside his major project—the writing of the third volume of *Una Storia Italiana*—and began working on a novel entitled *La costanza della ragione* (Verona, 1963). In this novel Pratolini adheres closely to the principles of literary realism that he has expounded theoretically in several significant articles and practiced in *Metello* and *Lo scialo*: It is a "private story" of the moral and spiritual education of a "typical" young worker set against the background of Italian society during the period 1941 to 1960; the novel is embedded in historical fact, and attempts to relate the personal feelings and experiences of the main characters to the decisively important political events of the time.

Indeed, *La costanza dela ragione* develops themes and characters that predominate not only in *Metello* and *Lo scialo* but that manifest themselves in various ways in all of Pratolini's works. Like the main characters of "La Prima età," *Via de' Magazzini, Il Quartiere, Cronache* and *Metello*, Bruno Santini, the protagonist of *La costanza dela ragione*, undergoes a process of gradual development which is conditioned by his own inner need to understand himself and the world in which he lives, and by the forces of social progress and reaction that impinge themselves upon him at every stage of his life. Like all of Pratolini's works since *Il Quartiere* in 1944, *La costanza della ragione* is intensely involved with problems of political and moral commitment. Bruno's decision to join the Communist Party at the end of the novel is motivated by a whole series of complex factors, not the least of which is his inability to find any other rational alternative in present-day Italy to the programs and solutions proposed by the Italian communists. But *La costanza della ragione* is not primarily a political novel, for Pratolini remains tied in this work to another constant aspect of his conception of life and of literary realism, namely the conviction that the deepest springs of human action draw their sustenance from emotional sources. At the vital center of *La costanza della ragione* is the story of Bruno's relationships with his mother, Ivana, with his mentor, Milloschi, a communist worker and ex-partisan, and above all with his sweetheart, Lori, an honest, vivacious, perceptive young woman whose death forces Bruno to re-examine everything in which he believes and holds sacred.

If *La constanza della ragione* is any indication of the path that Pratolini will follow in the future, we can expect him to remain firmly committed to the theory and practice of social realism which have guided him during the past fifteen years. What can be said with certainty is that, on the basis of his solid achievement from *Il Quartiere* to *La costanza della ragione*, Pratolini has acquired a prominent position among European novelists of the twentieth century who have concerned themselves in their art with the crucial problems and conflicts of our time.

1—The Early Years (1913–1932)

1. Most of the biographical material in this and succeeding chapters was obtained directly from Pratolini. I have also drawn some of my information from three of Pratolini's autobiographical books, *Il tappeto verde*, *Via de' Magazzini*, and *Cronaca familiare*, whose correspondence to the authentic facts of his early life was verified by Pratolini himself. In a few instances I have drawn information from other critics' published interviews with Pratolini.

2. These events are described by Pratolini in *Cronaca familiare* (Florence, 1947), pp. 35–37.

3. V.P., "Prima vita di Sapienza," *Letteratura*, October, 1938, 72.

2—The Young Fascist Writer (1932–1939)

1. From Pratolini's preface to "Diario di Villa Rosa," in *Il mio cuore a Ponte Milvio* (Rome, 1954).

2. The two years Pratolini spent working for the Fascist ministry did severe damage to his reputation at a later date. In the early part of February, 1944, the newspaper *Il Corriere della era* published a list of artists, writers, and journalists who had "sold out" to fascism. Pratolini's name appeared in the list. For a background of this incident, see Luigi Russo's essay on Pratolini in *I narratori* (Milan, 1951), pp. 366–69.

3. Alberto Carocci and Giansiro Ferrata, "Corsivo," *Solaria*, January, 1926, 1–3.

4. "Avvisi," *L'Universale*, June 3, 1931. 1. (Unsigned)

5. Among the other regular contributors to *Il Bargello*'s "third page" were Bruno Becchi, Romano Romanelli, Alberto Lucchini, Alessandro Pavolini, Raffaello Franchi, Ettore Allodoli, Walter Bartoli, and Elio Vittorini.

6. V.P., "Omaggio a Beccherini," *Il Bargello*, Nov. 25, 1934, 3.

7. V.P., "Coi Negadi in Etiopia," *Il Bargello*, Sept. 22, 1935, 3.

8. V.P., "Il soldato torna contadino," *Il Bargello*, August 2, 1936, 3.

9. V.P., "Tempo culturale della politica," *Il Bargello*, Jan. 31, 1937, 3.

10. Vittorini gave me this information, later confirmed by Pratolini, during the course of an interview in October, 1956.

11. V.P., "Crepuscoli," *Il Bargello*, Sept. 27, 1936, 1.

12. V.P., "Precisazioni sui fascismi stranieri." *Il Bargello*, Oct. 11, 1936, 1.

13. V.P., "Rosai fuori della polemica," *Il Bargello*, Nov. 21, 1937, 3.

14. V.P., "Pensieri di giovane," *Il Bargello*, July 31, 1932, 3.

15. V.P., "Richiamo," *Il Bargello*, Feb. 26, 1933, 3.

16. V.P., "La letteratura del tempo nostro," *Il Bargello*, June 9, 1935, 3.

17. V.P., "Giuliotti malpensante," *Il Bargello*, Sept. 3, 1936, 3.

18. Domenico Giuliotti, "Il merlo sulla forca," *Il Frontespizio*, Jan., 1933, 1.

19. V.P., "Come esempio," *Il Bargello*, Feb. 28, 1937, 3.

20. V.P., "Vita di Tozzi," *Il Bargello*, March 31, 1935, 3.

21. V.P., "Calendario," *Campo di Marte*, Aug. 1, 1938, 1.

22. V.P., "Calendario," *Campo di Marte*, Aug. 1, 1938, 1.

23. V.P., "Callegari, o del romanzo fascista," *Campo di Marte*, Aug. 15, 1938, 3.

24. V.P., "Calendario," *Campo di Marte*, Oct. 1, 1938, 2.

25. V.P., "Fantasia d'Estate," *Il Bargello*, Sept. 18, 1932, 3.

26. V.P., "Episodi," *Il Bargello*, Aug. 12, 1932, 3.

27. V.P., "Vent' anni di Uno," *Il Bargello*, March 24, 1935, 3.

28. V.P., "Racconto di un amore vero," *Il Bargello*, Sept. 23, 1934, 3.

29. V.P., "Gesuina," Aug. 8, 1937, 3.

30. "Early Childhood" comprises the first two parts of the story "Prima Vita di Sapienza," which was published in *Letteratura*, Oct., 1938, 69–75. Parts of "1917" (1937), "The Green Rug" (1938), "The Hand" (1937), and "A Memorable Day" (1936) first appeared in *Letteratura* and *Corrente*. Pratolini later selected these five works from among his early writings for publication in his first book, *Il tappeto verde* (Florence, 1941). All of the passages quoted in the following pages are taken from *Il tappeto verde*.

31. Pietro Pancrazi, "Poesia e verità di Pratolini," *Il Corriere della Sera*, March 9, 1948, 3.

3—Reminiscence and Remorse (1939–1943)

1. *Incontro, Rivoluzione, Letteratura, La Ruota, Corrente,* and *L'Ambrosiano.*

2. V.P., *Il tappeto verde* (Florence, 1941).

3. V.P., *Via de' Magazzini* (Florence, 1942).

4. Mario Pratesi, *L'Eredità* (Milan, 1942), edited and with a critical introduction by Vasco Pratolini.

5. V.P., *Le amiche* (Florence, 1943).

6. Tullio Cicciarelli, "Vasco Pratolini," *Il Secolo*, September 7, 1941, 3.

7. V.P., "Libri, riviste, giornali," *La Ruota*, May–July, 1942.

8. Enrico Falqui, *Prosatori e narratori del novecento italiano* (Turin, 1950), p. 410.

9. Franco Calamandrei, "Una generazione e un suo narratore," *Il Politecnico*, June, 1946, 35.

10. V.P., *Il tappeto verde*, pp. 65–67. First published in *Rivoluzione*, November 5, 1940, 3.

11. *Ibid.*, pp. 69–71. First published in *Incontro*, April 10, 1940, 3.

12. *Ibid.*, pp. 73–75. First published in *Rivoluzione*, with the title "In Memoriam," February 20, 1941, 3.

13. *Ibid.*, pp. 77–79. First published in *Incontro*, June 20, 1940, p. 3. (Italy declared war on England and France on June 11, 1940.)

14. *Ibid.*, p 74.

15. *Ibid.*, p. 73.

16. *Ibid.*, p. 75.

17. *Ibid.*, p. 69.

18. V.P., "Per Jahier," *Incontro*, February 25, 1940, 4.

19. V.P., "Voce sola," *Letteratura*, July–September, 1940, 145.

20. V.P., *Via de' Magazzini*, 2nd edition (Milan, 1949). The passages quoted in the following pages are taken from this edition.

21. V.P., *Le amiche* (Florence, 1943). The passages quoted in the following pages are taken from *Diario sentimentale* (Florence, 1956), an anthology of the autobiographical writings from 1936 to 1946.

22. V.P., "Callegari, o del romanzo fascista," *Campo di Marte*, October, 1938, 2.

4—The Discovery of the Human Community
(1943–1950)

1. *Lettere di condannati a morte della resistenza italiana,* ed. Enzo Enriques Agnoletti (Turin, 1955), p. 182.

2. Giaime Pintor, *Il sangue d'Europa* (Turin, 1950), pp. 247–248.

3. The Italian government's surrender to the Allies on September 8, 1943, precipitated the beginning of civil war in Italy, since German troops immediately swept down into Italy, forcing an irreparable break between those Italians who were still loyal to Mussolini and to fascism, and those who chose to align themselves with the anti-Fascist and anti-Nazi Resistance.

4. V.P., "I compagni," written in February, 1945, and published in *Il mio cuore a Ponte Milvio* (Rome, 1945), p. 66.

5. V.P., "La primula rossa alla tomba di Nerone," *Diario sentimentale* (Florence, 1956), p. 272.

6. V.P., "Settore Flaminio Ponte Milvio," *Mercurio*, December, 1944, 157.

7. *Inchiesta sul neorealismo* (Turin, 1951), p. 17.

8. *Ibid.*, p. 13.

9. *Ibid.*, pp. 88–89.

10. Excluding the works of Pratolini, among the best known neo-realist novels dealing with the themes of war, political conflict, and social disorder are: Elio Vittorini, *Uomini e no* (Milan, 1945); Renata Viganò, *L'Agnese va a morire* (Turin, 1949); Italo Calvino, *Il sentiero dei nidi di ragno* (Turin, 1947); Cesare Pavese, *Il compagno* (Turin, 1947); Francesco Jovine, *L'impero in provincia* (Rome, 1945); Giuseppe Berto, *Il cielo è rosso* (Milan, 1947); Guido Piovene, *Pietà contro pietà* (Milan, 1946); Giovanni Commisso, *Gioventù che muore* (Milan, 1949); and Carlo Levi, *L'orologio* (Turin, 1950).

11. V.P., "Cronache di poveri amanti," *Il Corriere del Libro*, February 17, 1947. The "dialogue" to which Pratolini refers in this article is *Cronaca familiare*, a short autobiographical book he wrote in December, 1945, in memory of his brother Ferruccio, who died in July, 1945, at the age of twenty-seven.

12. V.P., "Vita popolare fiorentina," *Le Vie d'Italia*, January, 1949, 57.

13. Dino Compagni, *Cronica delle cose occorrenti ne' tempi suoi*, in *Cronisti del Trecento*, ed. Roberto Palmarocchi (Milan-Rome, 1935), pp. 79, 150.

14. The influence of Lermontov and Moravia is explained at the beginning of my discussion of *Un eroe del nostro tempo*.

15. Victor Hugo, *Choses Vues*, ed. and trans. Vasco Pratolini (Turin, 1943).

16. Eugenio Montale, "Un romanzo popolista," *Il Mondo*, May 5, 1945, 6.

17. Charles Louis Philippe, *Bubu de Montparnasse*, trans. Vasco Pratolini (Rome, 1944).

18. V.P., *Il Quartiere* (Milan, 1944). The passages quoted in the following pages are taken from the translation of Peter and Pamela Duncan, *The Naked Streets* (New York, 1952).

19. V.P., *Cronaca familiare* (Florence, 1947). The passages quoted in the following pages are taken from Barbara

Kennedy's translation, *Two Brothers* (New York, 1962).

20. *Ibid.*, pp. 7, 8.

21. V.P., *Cronache di poveri amanti* (Florence, 1947). The passages quoted in the following pages are taken from the Viking Press translation (New York, 1949), owned by Hamish Hamilton Ltd.

22. V.P., "Cronache fiorentine 20' Secolo," *Il Politecnico*, December, 1947, 29.

23. V.P., *Un eroe del nostro tempo* (Milan, 1949). The passages quoted in the following pages are my translations based on the 2nd edition (Milan, 1954).

24. V.P., "Libri, riviste, giornali," *La Ruota*, Jan.–Feb., 1942.

25. V.P., "Società e romanzo," *Sempre Avanti!* December 21, 1947, 3.

26. In an interview with Carlo Bo, *L'Europeo*, June, 1960, 50.

27. The passages quoted in the following pages are taken from William Fense Weaver's translation, *The Girls of San Frediano* (New York, 1954).

28. Raffaele Viviani, *Poesie*, ed. Vasco Pratolini and Paolo Ricci (Florence, 1956), pp. 8–9.

29. Luigi Russo, *I narratori 1850–1950* (Milan, 1951), p. 372.

5—An Italian Tale (1950–1960)

1. V.P., *Metello* (Florence, 1955).

2. V.P., *Lo scialo*, 2 vols. (Verona, 1960).

3. V.P., "Questioni sul realismo," *Tempo Presente*, July, 1957, 523–27.

4. In an interview with Carlo Bo, *L'Europeo*, July, 1960, 50–54.

5. Interview with Carlo Bo, *L'Europeo*, July, 1960, 52.

6. V.P., "Metello Salani," *L'Edile*, January, 1956, 3.

7. The statements regarding the general premise of the trilogy, the statement of method and aim, the premise of *Metello*, and the premise of *Lo scialo* are taken from Pratolini's interview with Carlo Bo, *L'Europeo*, July, 1960, 50–54. The statement regarding the premise of *I fidanzati del Mugnone* is taken from Pratolini's interview with Mino Guerrini, *Epoca*, June, 1960, 20.

8. V.P., "Questioni sul realismo," *Tempo Presente*, July, 1957, 526.

9. V.P., *Metello* (Florence, 1955). The passages quoted in the following pages are my translations based on the 5th edition (Florence, 1955).

10. V.P., *Lo scialo*, two vols. (Verona, 1960). The passages quoted in the following pages are my translations based on this edition.

11. Interview with Carlo Bo, *L'Europeo*, July, 1960, 52.

12. The verb *scialare* has three separate, albeit closely interrelated meanings: 1) to dissipate, to squander; 2) to enjoy oneself in frivolous amusements: 3) to be decomposed or broken up. Only the first two expressions are currently in use.

13. Interview with Carlo Bo, *L'Europeo*, July, 1960, 54.

14. *Ibid.*

A SELECTED BIBLIOGRAPHY

Agnoletti, Enzo Enriques, ed. *Lettere di condannati a morte della Resistenza italiana.* Einaudi, Turin, 1955.

Anceschi, Luciano, and Sergio Antonelli, ed. *Lirica del novecento.* Vallecchi, Florence, 1953.

Angioletti, G. B., and G. Antonini, ed. *Narratori italiani d'oggi.* Vallecchi, Florence, 1939.

Asor Rosa, Alberto, *Vasco Pratolini.* Edizioni Moderne, Rome, 1958.

Battaglia, Roberto, *Storia della Resistenza italiana.* Einaudi, Turin, 1953.

Bo, Carlo, ed. *Inchiesta sul neorealismo.* Edizioni Radio Italiana, Turin, 1951.

Bottai, Giuseppe, *Politica fascista delle arti.* Angelo Signorelli, Rome, 1940.

Chiarini, Luigi, *Fascismo e letteratura.* Istituto Nazionale di Cultura, Rome, 1936.

Devoto, Giacomo, *Profilo di storia linguistica italiana.* La Nuova Italia, Florence, 1954.

Falqui, Enrico, *Novecento letterario.* Vallecchi, Florence, 1954.

———. *Prosatori e narratori del novecento italiano.* Einaudi, Turin, 1950.

Fernandez, Dominque, *Il romanzo italiano e la crisi della coscienza moderna.* Lerici, Milan, 1960.

Flora, Francesco, *Scrittori italiani contemporanei.* Nistri Lischi, Pisa, 1952.

———. *Storia della letteratura italiana.* Vol. 3. Mondadori, Verona, 1948.

Gargiulo, Alfredo, *La letteratura italiana del novecento.* Felice Le Monnier, Florence, 1940.

Guarnieri, Silvio, *Cinquant'anni di narrativa in Italia*. Parenti, Florence, 1954.

Longobardi, Fulvio, *Vasco Pratolini*. Mursia, Milan, 1964.

Lukacs, Gyorgy, *Saggi sul realismo*. Einaudi, Turin, 1950.

Pacifici, Sergio, *A Guide to Contemporary Italian Literature*. The World Publishing Company, Cleveland, 1962.

Paoluzi, Angelo, *La letteratura della Resistenza*. Edizioni Cinque Lune, Florence, 1956.

Pintor, Giaime, *Il sangue d'Europa*. Einaudi, Turin, 1950.

Pullini, Giorgio, *Il romanzo italiano del dopoguerra*. Schwarz, Milan, 1961.

Raya, Gino, *Storia dei generi letterari: il romanzo*. Francesco Vallardi, Milan, 1950.

Romano, Salvatore Francesco, *Poetica dell'ermetismo*. Sansoni, Florence, 1942.

Rondi, Brunello, *Il neorealismo italiano*. Guanda, Parma, 1956.

Russo, Luigi, *I narratori 1850–1950*. Giuseppe Principato, Milan, 1951.

Sapegno, Natalino, *Disegno storico della letteratura italiana*. La Nuova Italia, Florence, 1949.

Seroni, Adriano, *Ragioni critiche*. Vallecchi, Florence, 1944.

Spagnoletti, Giacinto, *Romanzieri italiani del nostro secolo*. Edizioni Radio Italiana, Turin, 1957.

Sticco, Maria, *Il romanzo italiano contemporaneo: 1920–1950*. Vita e Pensiero, Rome, 1953.

Vittorini, Domenico, *The Modern Italian Novel*. University of Pennsylvania Press, Philadelphia, 1930.

Vittorini, Elio, preface to *Il garofano rosso*. Mondadori, Verona, 1948.

INDEX